Bertolt Brecht: Plays, Poetry and Prose
Edited by JOHN WILLETT *and* RALPH MANHEIM

Poems 1913–1956

Part Three 1938–1956

Bertolt Brecht Poems

Edited by JOHN WILLETT *and* RALPH MANHEIM
with the co-operation of Erich Fried

Part Three 1938–1956

LONDON
Eyre Methuen

ISBN 0 413 34560 2

*Printed in Great Britain
by Richard Clay (The Chaucer Press) Ltd., Bungay, Suffolk.*

Contents

THE TRANSLATORS

Edith Anderson · Derek Bowman · Lee Baxendall ·
Patrick Bridgwater · Martin Esslin · H. R. Hays ·
Michael Hamburger · Frank Jellinek · Nicholas Jacobs ·
H. Arthur Klein · Lesley Lendrum · Christopher Middleton ·
Humphrey Milne · Sammy McLean · Edith Roseveare ·
George Rapp · Naomi Replansky · John Willett.

Editors' Note

For this paperback edition, the Brecht *Poems* have been split into three parts. The first contains our selection up to 1928 (the year of *The Three-penny Opera*); the second continues it up to 1938 (i.e. from the world economic crisis to the eve of the war); while the third contains the remainder, up to his death in 1956. Since the hardback volume from which all three derive is comprised in the general English-language edition of Brecht's work, those poems which occur elsewhere (i.e. primarily in the plays) are excluded. A fourth, companion paperback will contain a selection from them, and this will cover the whole time-span.

The pages of the present edition are numbered as in the hardback. However, it excludes the critical apparatus of that large volume: i.e. Brecht's own notes and comments on poetry, the note on 'The principal collections of Brecht's poems' (relating the poems to his sometimes un-realised plans for grouping and collecting them), and the fairly detailed notes on separate poems, which also give particulars of musical settings. The hardback volume also contains a much fuller introduction. Anybody seeking this information will have to consult the hardback volume. The paperbacks give the poems without explanation or comment.

The principles behind the selection, the general method of translation and the decision not to print the German originals are explained in the hardback introduction. The basic text followed is that of the 1967 Ger-man collected edition (major variations being shown in the notes). However, unlike the original editors we have tried to follow a chrono-logical arrangement. The aim is to show the development of Brecht's poetry and its close relationship with the times through which he lived.

VII The Darkest Times
1938–1941

Five Visions

I stood on a hill and I saw the Old approaching, but it came as the New.

It hobbled up on new crutches which no one had ever seen before and stank of new smells of decay which no one had ever smelt before.

The stone that rolled past was the newest invention and the screams of the gorillas drumming on their chests set up to be the newest musical composition.

Everywhere you could see open graves standing empty as the New advanced on the capital.

Round about stood such as inspired terror, shouting: Here comes the New, it's all new, salute the New, be new like us! And those who heard, heard nothing but their shouts, but those who saw, saw such as were not shouting.

So the Old strode in disguised as the New, but it brought the New with it in its triumphal procession and presented it as the Old.

The New went fettered and in rags; they revealed its splendid limbs.

And the procession moved through the night, but what they thought was the light of dawn was the light of fires in the sky. And the cry: Here comes the New, it's all new, salute the New, be new like us! would have been easier to hear if all had not been drowned in a thunder of guns.

GREAT BABEL GIVES BIRTH

When her time was come she withdrew into her innermost
chamber and surrounded herself with doctors and soothsayers.

There was whispering. Solemn men went into the house
with grave faces and came out with anxious faces that were
pale. And the price of white make-up doubled in the beauty
shops.

In the street the people gathered and stood from morning
till night with empty stomachs.

The first sound that was heard was like a mighty fart in the
rafters, followed by a mighty cry of PEACE!, whereupon the
stink became greater.

Immediately after that, blood spurted up in a thin watery
jet. And now came further sounds in unceasing succession,
each more terrible than the last.

Great Babel vomited and it sounded like FREEDOM! and
coughed and it sounded like JUSTICE! and farted again and
it sounded like PROSPERITY! And wrapped in a bloody sheet
a squalling brat was carried on to the balcony and shown to
the people with ringing of bells, and it was WAR.

And it had a thousand fathers.

THE DISPUTE (A.D. 1938)

I saw them stand on four hills. Two yelled and two were
silent. All were surrounded by their retainers, animals and
wares. All the servants on all four hills were pale and lean.
All four were enraged. Two held knives in their hands, and
two carried knives in the shafts of their boots.

'Give us back what you stole from us,' two of them yelled,
'or there will be a disaster.' And two were silent, nonchalantly
observing the weather.

'We are hungry,' two yelled, 'but we are armed.' At that the
two others began to speak.

'What we took from you was worthless and small and didn't

satisfy your hunger,' they said with dignity. 'Well, hand it back, then, if it isn't worth anything,' the two others yelled. 'We don't like the look of those knives,' said the dignified men. 'Put them away and you'll get something.' – 'Vain promises,' the hungry men yelled. 'When we didn't have knives you didn't even make promises.'

'Why don't you make useful goods?' asked the dignified men.

'Because you won't let us sell them,' the hungry men answered angrily; 'that's why we made knives.'

Yet they were not hungry themselves, so they kept pointing at their retainers, who were hungry. And the dignified men said to each other: 'Our retainers too are hungry.'

And they came down from their hills to negotiate, so that the yelling would cease, for there were too many hungry men. And the two others also came down from their hills and the conversation became quiet.

'Between ourselves,' two of them said, 'we live on our retainers.' And two nodded their heads, saying: 'And so do we.'

'If we don't get anything,' the bellicose men said, 'we shall send out our retainers against yours, and you will be beaten.'

'Perhaps it's you that will be beaten,' smiled the pacific men.

'Yes, perhaps we shall be beaten,' said the bellicose men. 'Then our retainers will pounce on us and kill us and discuss with your retainers how to kill you. For when the masters don't speak to one another the retainers speak to one another.'

'What is it you need?' asked the pacific men, startled. And the bellicose men produced long lists from their pockets.

But all four stood up like one man and turned to all the retainers and said in a loud voice: 'We shall now discuss ways of maintaining peace.'

And sat down and looked at the lists, and they were too long. So that the pacific men flushed with rage and said: 'We see, you want to live on our retainers too,' and they returned to their hills.

Then the bellicose ones also returned to their hills.

I saw them stand on four hills and all four were yelling. All four held knives in their hands and said to their retainers: 'Those people over there want you to work for them. Only war can settle it.'

THE STONE FISHERMAN

The big fisherman has appeared again. He sits in his rotted boat and fishes from the time when the first lamps flare up early in the morning until the last one is put out in the evening.

The villagers sit on the gravel of his embankment and watch him, grinning. He fishes for herring but he pulls up nothing but stones.

They all laugh. The men slap their sides, the women hold on to their bellies, the children leap high into the air with laughter.

When the big fisherman raises his torn net high and finds the stones in it, he does not hide them but reaches far out with his strong brown arms, seizes the stone, holds it high and shows it to the unlucky ones.

THE GOD OF WAR

I saw the old god of war stand in a bog between chasm and rockface.

He smelled of free beer and carbolic and showed his testicles to adolescents, for he had been rejuvenated by several professors. In a hoarse wolfish voice he declared his love for everything young. Nearby stood a pregnant woman, trembling.

And without shame he talked on and presented himself as a great one for order. And he described how everywhere he put barns in order, by emptying them.

And as one throws crumbs to sparrows, he fed poor people with crusts of bread which he had taken away from poor people.

His voice was now loud, now soft, but always hoarse.

In a loud voice he spoke of great times to come, and in a soft voice he taught the women how to cook crows and sea-gulls. Meanwhile his back was unquiet, and he kept looking round, as though afraid of being stabbed.

And every five minutes he assured his public that he would take up very little of their time.

THE WORLD'S ONE HOPE

1 Is oppression as old as the moss around ponds?
The moss around ponds is not avoidable.
Perhaps everything I see is natural, and I am sick and want to
remove what cannot be removed?
I have read songs of the Egyptians, of their men who built
the pyramids. They complained of their loads and asked when
oppression would cease. That's four thousand years ago.
Oppression, it would seem, is like the moss and unavoidable.

2 When a child is about to be run down by a car one pulls
it on to the pavement.
Not the kindly man does that, to whom they put up
monuments.
Anyone pulls the child away from the car.
But here many have been run down, and many pass by and
do nothing of the sort.
Is that because it's so many who are suffering? Should one not
help them all the more because they are many? One helps
them less. Even the kindly walk past and after that are as
kindly as ever they were before walking past.

3 The more there are suffering, then, the more natural their
sufferings appear. Who wants to prevent the fishes in the sea
from getting wet?
And the suffering themselves share this callousness towards
themselves and are lacking in kindness towards themselves.
It is terrible that human beings so easily put up with existing
conditions, not only with the sufferings of strangers but also
with their own.
All those who have thought about the bad state of things
refuse to appeal to the compassion of one group of people for
another. But the compassion of the oppressed for the
oppressed is indispensable.
It is the world's one hope.

THE CRUTCHES

Seven years I could not walk a step.
When I to the great physician came
He demanded: Why the crutches?
And I told him: I am lame.

He replied: That's not surprising.
Be so good and try once more.
If you're lame, it's these contraptions.
Fall then! Crawl across the floor!

And he took my lovely crutches
Laughing with a fiend's grimace
Broke them both across my back and
Threw them in the fireplace.

Well, I'm cured now: I can walk.
Cured by nothing more than laughter.
Sometimes, though, when I see sticks
I walk worse for some hours after.

LOVE SONG IN A BAD TIME

We had no friendly feelings for each other
Yet we made love like any other pair.
When we lay in each other's arms at night
The moon was less a stranger than you were.

And if today I met you in the market
And both bought fish, it might provoke a fight:
We had no friendly feelings for each other
When we lay in each other's arms at night.

THE CONSEQUENCES OF PRUDENCE

I hear you want to
Turn your car again at the same place
Where you once before turned it. The ground there
Was firm.
Don't you do it. Remember
Because you turned your car
There are ruts in the ground. Now
Your car will get stuck there.

SONNET NO. 19

My one requirement: that you stay with me.
I want to hear you, grumble as you may.
If you were deaf I'd need what you might say
If you were dumb I'd need what you might see.

If you were blind I'd want you in my sight
For you're the sentry posted to my side:
We're hardly half way through our lengthy ride
Remember we're surrounded yet by night.

Your 'let me lick my wounds' is no excuse now.
Your 'anywhere' (not here) is no defence
There'll be relief for you, but no release now.

You know whoever's needed can't go free
And you are needed urgently by me
I speak of me when us would make more sense.

BAD TIME FOR POETRY

Yes, I know: only the happy man
Is liked. His voice
Is good to hear. His face is handsome.

The crippled tree in the yard
Shows that the soil is poor, yet
The passers-by abuse it for being crippled
And rightly so.

The green boats and the dancing sails on the Sound
Go unseen. Of it all
I see only the torn nets of the fishermen.
Why do I only record
That a village woman aged forty walks with a stoop?
The girls' breasts
Are as warm as ever.

In my poetry a rhyme
Would seem to me almost insolent.

Inside me contend
Delight at the apple tree in blossom
And horror at the house-painter's speeches.
But only the second
Drives me to my desk.

IS THE PEOPLE INFALLIBLE?

1
My teacher
Tall and kindly
Has been shot, condemned by a people's court
As a spy. His name is damned.
His books are destroyed. Talk about him
Is suspect and suppressed.
Suppose he is innocent?

2
The sons of the people have found him guilty
The factories and collective farms of the workers

The world's most heroic institutions
Have identified him as an enemy.
No voice has been raised for him.
Suppose he is innocent?

3

The people has many enemies.
In the highest places
Sit enemies. In the most useful laboratories
Sit enemies. They build
Dykes and canals for the good of whole continents, and the
    canals
Silt up and the dykes
Collapse. The man in charge has to be shot.
Suppose he is innocent?

4

The enemy goes disguised.
He pulls a workman's cap over his eyes. His friends
Know him as a conscientious worker. His wife
Shows his leaky shoes
Worn out in the people's service.
And yet he is an enemy. Was my teacher one of them?
Suppose he is innocent?

5

To speak of the enemies that may be sitting in the people's
    courts
Is dangerous, for courts have reputations to keep up.
To ask for papers proving guilt in black and white
Is senseless, for there need be no such papers.
The criminals have proofs of their innocence to hand.
The innocent often have no proof.
Is it best to keep silent then?
Suppose he is innocent?

6

What 5000 have built one man can destroy.
Of 50 condemned
One may be guiltless.
Suppose he is innocent?

7

Suppose he is innocent
How will he go to his death?

MOTTO

Seated up in the boat's bows, as you
Notice the leak down at the other end
Better not turn your eyes away, my friend
For you are not outside Death's field of view.

SWEDISH LANDSCAPE

Beneath the grey pine trees a crumbling house.
Amid rubble a white-lacquered chest.
An altar? A counter? That is the question.
Was the body of Jesus sold here? His blood
On draught? Or linen celebrated, and boots?
Was earthly or heavenly profit made here?
Did clerics trade here or tradesmen preach?
God's lovely creation, the pine trees
Are sold off by the locksmith next door.

IN PRAISE OF DOUBT

Praised be doubt! I advise you to greet
Cheerfully and with respect the man

Who tests your word like a bad penny.
I'd like you to be wise and not to give
Your word with too much assurance.

Read history and see
The headlong flight of invincible armies.
Wherever you look
Impregnable strongholds collapse and
Even if the Armada was innumerable as it left port
The returning ships
Could be numbered.

Thus one day a man stood on the unattainable summit
And a ship reached the end of
The endless sea.

O beautiful the shaking of heads
Over the indisputable truth!
O brave the doctor's cure
Of the incurable patient!

But the most beautiful of all doubts
Is when the downtrodden and despondent raise their heads
        and
Stop believing in the strength
Of their oppressors.

*   *   *

Oh, how laboriously the new truth was fought for!
What sacrifices it cost!
How difficult it was to see
That things were thus and not thus!
With a sigh of relief one day a man entered it in the record of
        knowledge.
For a long time perhaps it stands there, and many generations
Live with it and regard it as eternal wisdom
And the learned scorn all who are ignorant of it.

And then it may happen that a suspicion arises, for new
      experience
Makes the established truth open to question. Doubt spreads
And then one day a man thoughtfully strikes it out
From the record of knowledge.

Deafened by commands, examined
For his fitness to fight by bearded doctors, inspected
By resplendent creatures with golden insignia, admonished
By solemn clerics who throw at him a book written by God
      himself
Instructed
By impatient schoolmasters, stands the poor man and is told
That the world is the best of worlds and that the hole
In the roof of his hovel was planned by God in person.
Truly he finds it hard
To doubt this world.

*　　　*　　　*

There are the thoughtless who never doubt.
Their digestion is splendid, their judgement infallible.
They don't believe in the facts, they believe only in them-
      selves. When it comes to the point
The facts must go by the board. Their patience with
      themselves
Is boundless. To arguments
They listen with the ear of a police spy.

The thoughtless who never doubt
Meet the thoughtful who never act.
They doubt, not in order to come to a decision but
To avoid a decision. Their heads
They use only for shaking. With anxious faces
They warn the crews of sinking ships that water is dangerous.
Beneath the murderer's axe
They ask themselves if he isn't human too.
Murmuring something

About the situation not yet being clarified, they go to bed.
Their only action is to vacillate.
Their favourite phrase is: not yet ripe for discussion.

*   *   *

Therefore, if you praise doubt
Do not praise
The doubt which is a form of despair.

What use is the ability to doubt to a man
Who can't make up his mind?
He who is content with too few reasons
May act wrongly
But he who needs too many
Remains inactive under danger.

You who are a leader of men, do not forget
That you are that because you doubted other leaders.
So allow the led
Their right to doubt.

ON EASE

Just see the ease
With which the powerful
River tears down its banks!
The earthquake shakes the ground
With indolent hand.
The terrible fire
Gracefully reaches for the town's many houses
And devours them at leisure:
A polished eater.

ON THE JOY OF BEGINNING

Oh joy of beginning! Oh early morning!
First grass, when none remembers
What green looks like. Oh first page of the book
Long awaited, the surprise of it. Read it
Slowly, all too soon the unread part
Will be too thin for you. And the first splash of water
On a sweaty face! The fresh
Cool shirt. Oh the beginning of love! Glance that strays
      away!
Oh the beginning of work! Pouring oil
Into the cold machine. First touch and first hum
Of the engine springing to life! And first drag
Of smoke filling the lungs! And you too
New thought!

SONG ABOUT THE GOOD PEOPLE

1
One knows the good people by the fact
That they get better
When one knows them. The good people
Invite one to improve them, for
How does anyone get wiser? By listening
And by being told something.

2
At the same time, however
They improve anybody who looks at them and anybody
They look at. It is not just because they help one
To get jobs or to see clearly, but because
We know that these people are alive and are
Changing the world, that they are of use to us.

3

If one comes to them they are there.
They remember what they
Looked like when one last met them.
However much they've changed –
For it is precisely they who change –
They have at most become more recognisable.

4

They are like a house which we helped to build
They do not force us to live there
Sometimes they do not let us.
We may come to them at any time in our smallest dimension,
        but
What we bring with us we must select.

5

They know how to give reasons for their presents
If they find them thrown away they laugh.
But here too they are reliable, in that
Unless we rely on ourselves
They cannot be relied on.

6

When they make mistakes we laugh:
For if they lay a stone in the wrong place
We, by watching them, see
The right place.
Daily they earn our interest, even as they earn
Their daily bread.
They are interested in something
That is outside themselves.

7

The good people keep us busy
They don't seem to be able to finish anything by themselves
All their solutions still contain problems.

At dangerous moments on sinking ships
Suddenly we see their eyes full on us.
Though they do not entirely approve of us as we are
They are in agreement with us none the less.

Five Theatre Poems

THE THEATRE, HOME OF DREAMS

Many see the theatre as a place for
Generating dreams. You actors are seen as
Dealers in narcotic drugs. In your darkened houses
People are changed into kings, and perform
Heroic deeds without risk. Gripped by enthusiasm
For oneself or sympathy with oneself
One sits in happy distraction, forgetting
The difficulties of daily life – a fugitive.
All kinds of stories are stirred together by your skilled hands
    so as to
Arouse our emotions. To that end you use
Incidents from the real world. Anyone, it is true
Who came into all this with the sounds of the traffic still in
    his ears
And still sober, would hardly recognise
Up there on your stage, the world he had just left.
And on stepping out of your houses after the end, moreover
A lowly man once more and no longer a king
He would no longer recognise the world, and would feel
Displaced in real life.
Many, it is true, see this activity as harmless. Given the
    ignominy
And uniformity of our life, they say, we find
Dreams welcome. How can life be borne without
Dreams? But this, actors, makes your theatre
A place where one learns how to
Bear our ignominious and uniform
Life, and to give up not only
Great deeds but even sympathy with
Oneself. You, however
Show a false world, heedlessly stirred together

Just as dreams show it, transformed by wishes
Or twisted by fears, you miserable
Deceivers.

SHOWING HAS TO BE SHOWN

Show that you are showing! Among all the varied attitudes
Which you show when showing how men play their parts
The attitude of showing must never be forgotten.
All attitudes must be based on the attitude of showing
This is how to practise: before you show the way
A man betrays someone, or is seized by jealousy
Or concludes a deal, first look
At the audience, as if you wished to say:
'Now take note, this man is now betraying someone and this
        is how he does it.
This is what he is like when jealousy seizes him, and this
Is how he deals when dealing.' In this way
Your showing will keep the attitude of showing
Of putting forward what has been made ready, of finishing off
Of continually going further. So show
That what you show is something you show every night,
        have often shown before
And your playing will resemble a weaver's weaving, the
        work of a
Craftsman. And all that goes with showing
Like your continual concern to
Make watching simpler, always to ensure the best
View of every episode – that too you should make visible.
        Then
All this betraying and dealing and
Being seized by jealousy will be as it were
Imbued with something of the quality of a
Daily operation, for instance of eating, saying Good Morning
        and

Doing one's work. (For you are working, aren't you?) And
     behind your
Stage parts you yourselves must still be visible, as those who
Are playing them.

ON SPEAKING THE SENTENCES

And I so arranged the sentences that their effects
Became visible, I mean in such a way that
The fact of speaking them could
Make the speaker happy, or unhappy, and we others too
Could be made unhappy, or happy, by hearing him speak
     thus.
(Hence the plays became harder to see: the first
Impression often sank in only when they were seen the
     second time.)

THE MOMENT BEFORE IMPACT

I speak my lines before
The audience hears them; what they will hear is
Something done with. Every word that leaves the lip
Describes an arc, and then
Falls on the listener's ear; I wait and hear
The way it strikes; I know
We are not feeling the same thing and
We are not feeling it at the same time.

THE PLAY IS OVER

The play is over. The performance committed. Slowly
The theatre, a sagging intestine, empties. In the dressing
     rooms
The nimble salesmen of hotchpotch mimicry, of rancid
     rhetoric

Wash off make-up and sweat. At last
The lights go down which showed up the miserable
Botched job; twilight falls on the
Lovely nothingness of the misused stage. In the empty
Still mildly smelly auditorium sits the honest
Playwright, unappeased, and does his best
To remember.

LITERATURE WILL BE SCRUTINISED

For Martin Andersen Nexö

I

Those who have been set on golden chairs to write
Will be questioned about those who
Wove their coats.
Not for their elevated thoughts
Will their books be scrutinised, but
Any casual phrase that suggests
Something about those who wove coats
Will be read with interest, for it may involve characteristics
Of famous ancestors.

Whole literatures
Couched in the choicest expressions
Will be examined for signs
That revolutionaries too lived where there was oppression.
Pleading appeals to immortal beings
Will prove that at that time mortals sat over other mortals.
The delicious music of words will only relate
That for many there was no food.

II

But at that time will be praised
Those who sat on the bare ground to write
Those who sat among the lowly
Those who sat with the fighters.
Those who reported the sufferings of the lowly
Those who reported the deeds of the fighters
With art. In the noble words
Formerly reserved
For the adulation of kings.

Their accounts of abuses and their manifestos
Will still bear the thumb-mark
Of the lowly. For to these
They were transmitted; and they
Carried them on under their sweat-soaked shirts
Through the police cordons
To their fellows.

Yes, a time will come when
These clever and friendly men
These angry and hopeful men
Who sat on the bare ground to write
Who were surrounded by the lowly and the fighters
Will be publicly praised.

ARDENS SED VIRENS

Splendid, what the lovely fire
Cannot turn to chilly ash!
Sister, you're my heart's desire
Burning, and yet still intact.

Many I saw slyly cooling
Hotheads stunned by ignoring fact.
Sister, you repay my schooling
Burning, and yet still intact.

In the battle you'd no horse on
Which to ride off when attacked
So I watched you fight with caution
Burning, and yet still intact.

SONNET NO. 1

And now it's war; our path is growing steeper.
You, my companion sent to share the journey

On broad or narrow roads, on smooth or stony
A student each of us, and each a teacher

And each now fleeing for the selfsame end
Know what I know: This end cannot be counted
More than the journey, so that if one fainted
And if the other left him, all intent

To gain his end, why, it would surely vanish
Not to be seen again, or found by asking.
Breathless he'd run until he stood in panic

Sweating, in grey and neutral nothingness.
To tell you this, and mark the point we're passing
I put my message in poetic dress.

ON GERMANY

You pleasant Bavarian forests, you cities on the Main
Spruce-covered Hesse mountains and you, shadowy Black
    Forest
You shall remain.
Thuringia's reddish screes, Brandenburg's frugal scrub
You black Ruhr cities, with your traffic of iron barges, why
Should you not remain?
And you, many-citied Berlin
Busy above and below the asphalt, may remain and you
Hanseatic ports shall remain and Saxony's
Teeming towns, you shall remain and you of Silesia
Wreathed in smoke, looking east, shall remain.
Only the scum of generals, gauleiters
Only the lords of factories, stockbrokers
Only the landlords, bailiffs – these are to go.
Sky and earth and wind and all that was made by man
Can remain, but
The filth, the exploiters – that
Cannot remain.

MOTTO

This, then, is all. It's not enough, I know.
At least I'm still alive, as you may see.
I'm like the man who took a brick to show
How beautiful his house used once to be.

1940

I
Spring is coming. The gentle winds
Are freeing the cliffs of their winter ice.
Trembling, the peoples of the north await
The battle fleets of the house-painter.

II
Out of the libraries
Emerge the butchers.
Pressing their children closer
Mothers stand and humbly search
The skies for the inventions of learned men.

III
The designers sit
Hunched in the drawing offices:
One wrong figure, and the enemy's cities
Will remain undestroyed.

IV
Fog envelops
The road
The poplars
The farms and
The artillery.

V

I am now living on the small island of Lidingö.
But one night recently
I had heavy dreams and I dreamed I was in a city
And discovered that its street signs
Were in German. I awoke
Bathed in sweat, saw the fir tree
Black as night before my window, and realised with relief:
I was in a foreign land.

VI

My young son asks me: Should I learn mathematics?
What for, I'm inclined to say. That two bits of bread are
          more than one
You'll notice anyway.
My young son asks me: Should I learn French?
What for, I'm inclined to say. That empire is going under.
Just rub your hand across your belly and groan
And you'll be understood all right.
My young son asks me: Should I learn history?
What for, I'm inclined to say. Learn to stick your head in the
          ground
Then maybe you'll come through.

Yes, learn mathematics, I tell him
Learn French, learn history!

VII

In front of the whitewashed wall
Stands the black military case with the manuscripts.
On it lie the smoking things with the copper ashtrays.
The Chinese scroll depicting the Doubter
Hangs above it. The masks are there too. And by the bedstead
Stands the little six-valve radio.
Mornings

I turn it on and hear
The victory bulletins of my enemies.

VIII

Fleeing from my fellow-countrymen
I have now reached Finland. Friends
Whom yesterday I didn't know, put up some beds
In clean rooms. Over the radio
I hear the victory bulletins of the scum of the earth. Curiously
I examine a map of the continent. High up in Lapland
Towards the Arctic Ocean
I can still see a small door.

IN THE BATH

The cabinet minister lies in his bath. With one hand he tries
To force the wooden brush below the glassy surface.
This childish play
Hides a serious core.

FINLAND 1940

I

We are now refugees in
Finland.

My little daughter
Returns home in the evening complaining that no child
Will play with her. She is a German, and comes
From a nation of gangsters.

When I exchange loud words during a discussion
I am told to be quiet. The people here do not like

Loud words from someone
Who comes from a nation of gangsters.

When I remind my little daughter
That the Germans are a nation of gangsters
She is glad with me that they are not loved
And we laugh together.

II
I, who am descended from peasants
Detest seeing
Bread thrown away.
You can understand
How I hate their war.

III
Over a bottle of wine
Our Finnish friend described to us
How the war laid waste her cherry orchard.
The wine we are drinking comes from it, she said.
We emptied our glasses
In memory of the ravaged cherry orchard
And to reason.

IV
This is the year which people will talk about
This is the year which people will be silent about.

The old see the young die.
The foolish see the wise die.

The earth no longer produces, it devours.
The sky hurls down no rain, only iron.

IN TIMES OF EXTREME
PERSECUTION

Once you've been beaten
What will remain?
Hunger and sleet and
Driving rain.

Who'll point the lesson?
Just as of old
Hunger and cold
Will point the lesson.

Won't people say then
It could never have worked?
The heaviest laden
Will wish they had shirked.

What will remind them
Of all the killed?
Wounds still unhealed
Those will remind them.

TO A PORTABLE RADIO

You little box I carried on that trip
Concerned to save your works from getting broken
Fleeing from house to train, from train to ship
So I might hear the hated jargon spoken

Beside my bedside and to give me pain
Last thing at night, once more as dawn appears
Charting their victories and my worst fears:
Promise at least you won't go dead again!

TO THE DANISH REFUGE

O house between the Sound and the pear tree
That phrase THE TRUTH IS CONCRETE, long ago
Cemented in you by a refugee –
Has that survived the bombing, do you know?

PIPES

Abandoning, in haste to cross the border
My books to friends I ditched my poem too
But took my pipes, which broke the standing order
To refugees: Best have no things with you.

Those books mean little to a man who grim-
ly waits to see what gaolers are approaching.
His leather pouch and other kit for smoking
Now look like being of more help to him.

LARDER ON A FINNISH ESTATE, 1940

O shady store! The scent of dark green firs
Comes nightly swirling in to blend itself
With that of sweet milk from enormous churns
And smoky bacon on its cold stone shelf.

Beer, goats' milk cheese, new bread and berries
Picked from grey undergrowth heavy with dew . . .
To those fighting the war on empty bellies
Far to the south: I wish it were for you.

I READ ABOUT TANK BATTLES

You Augsburg dyer's son, once gamely striving
To match my skill at marbles long ago

Where are you now among the grey tanks driving
In clouds of dust to lay sweet Flanders low?

That bomb of flesh, chopped down above Calais
Was that the weaver's son whom I once knew?
Son of our baker in my childhood days
Was bleeding Artois's cry provoked by you?

FINNISH LANDSCAPE

Those fish-stocked waters! Lovely trees as well!
Such scents of berries and of birches there!
Thick-chorded winds that softly cradle air
As mild as though the clanking iron churns
Trundled from the white farmhouse were all left open!
Dizzy with sight and sound and thought and smell
The refugee beneath the alders turns
To his laborious job: continued hoping.

He notes the corn stooks, spots which beasts have strayed
Towards the lake, hears moos from their strong lungs
But also sees who's short of milk and corn.
He asks the boat that takes logs to be sawn:
Is that the way that wooden legs are made?
And sees a people silent in two tongues.

RUUSKANEN'S HORSE

When the world crisis entered its third winter
The peasants of Nivala felled trees as usual
And as usual the small horses dragged the timber
Down to the river, but this year
They got only five Finnmarks a trunk, as much as
A cake of soap costs. And when the fourth spring of the
    world crisis came

The cottages of those who had not paid their taxes that
       autumn were auctioned.
While those who had paid them could not buy the fodder
For their horses, without which they could not work field or
       forest
So that the horses' ribs stuck
Out of their lustreless hide. Then the Nivala headman
Came to the peasant Ruuskanen on his field and told him
With authority: 'Don't you know there's a law
Against cruelty to animals? Look at your horse. Its ribs
Are sticking out of its hide. This horse
Is sick, so it must be slaughtered.'
He went off on that. But when three days later
He passed by again, he saw Ruuskanen
With his scrawny horse in the minute field as if
Nothing had happened and there were no law and no headman.
Exasperated
He sent two gendarmes with strict orders
To take Ruuskanen's horse and
Lead the ill-used animal forthwith to the knacker's.
But the gendarmes, trailing
Ruuskanen's horse behind them through the village, saw as
       they looked round them
More and more peasants come running from the houses and
       steadily
Follow the horse, till at the end of the village
The gendarmes halted, uncertain, and the peasant Niskanen
A devout man, a friend of Ruuskanen's, made a proposal
That the village scrape together some fodder for the horse
So there would be no need for its slaughter. So the gendarmes
Returned to the animal-loving headman bringing no horse
       but
The peasant Niskanen with his glad tidings
For Ruuskanen's horse. 'Listen,' he said, 'headman
This horse is not sick, only lacks fodder and Ruuskanen
Will starve without his horse. Slaughter his horse and
You'll soon have to slaughter the man himself, Mr headman.'

'What kind of talk is that?' asked the headman. 'The horse
Is sick and the law is the law and that is why it'll be
        slaughtered.'
Troubled, the two gendarmes
Went back with Niskanen and
Took Ruuskanen's horse from Ruuskanen's stable and
Set about leading it to the knacker's; but
When they came to the edge of the village again, there stood
        fifty
Peasants like great stones and gazed
In silence at the two gendarmes. In silence
The pair left the mare behind at the edge of the village
And still in silence
The peasants of Nivala led Ruuskanen's mare back
To her stable.
'That's sedition,' said the headman. A day later
A dozen gendarmes with rifles arrived by train from Oulu
At Nivala, so pleasantly sited, so garlanded with meadows,
        just to prove that
The law is the law. That afternoon
The peasants took down from the scrubbed wall-beams
Their rifles hanging beside the panels painted
With biblical texts, the old rifles
From the 1918 civil war. Distributed to them
For use against the Reds. Now
They pointed them at the twelve gendarmes
From Oulu. The same evening
Three hundred peasants coming from many
Neighbouring villages besieged the house of the headman
On the hill not far from the church. Hesitantly
The headman went on the steps, waved a white hand and
Spoke eloquently about Ruuskanen's horse, promising
To spare its life; but the peasants
No longer spoke of Ruuskanen's horse but demanded
The end of forced auctions and that their taxes
Should be remitted. Scared to death the headman
Rushed to the telephone, for the peasants

Had forgotten not only that there was a law but also
That there was a telephone in the headman's house, and now
    he telephoned
His cry of distress to Helsinki, and that same night
There came from Helsinki, the capital, in seven buses
Two hundred soldiers with machine-guns and at the head of
    them
An armoured car. And with this military might
They defeated the peasants, beat them up in the village hall
Dragged their spokesmen before the court at Nivala and
    sentenced them
To a year and a half in prison, so that order
Might be restored in Nivala.
But of all of them in the sequel
Only Ruuskanen's horse was pardoned
By personal intervention of the Minister
In response to many letters from the public.

ODE TO A HIGH DIGNITARY

1
Exalted Vice-Consul, deign
To grant your quivering louse
The stamp that means happiness!

Sublime spirit
In whose image the gods were created
Suffer your inscrutable thoughts
To be interrupted for one second!

Four times
I succeeded in reaching your presence.
A few of my words
Thought up in sleepless nights
I hope have come close to you.

Twice I have had my hair cut for your sake
Never
Did I go to you hatless, my shabby cap
I always hid from you.

You know, your few words
Are interpreted for weeks by trembling families
For sinister hints or else for happy omens:
Is that why they are so cruel?

The great setter of traps approaches.
There is a small door, leading
Out of the trap. You
Have the key.
Will you throw it in?

2
Never fear, little man behind the desk!
Your superiors
Won't begrudge you the stamp.
In months of interrogation
You probed the applicant.
Every hair on his tongue is known to you.
Not one letter of your rules
Did you overlook. No question with a catch in it
Did you forget, now put an end to this torment!
Just bang that little stamp on, your superiors
Won't eat you up for that!

EARLY ON I LEARNED

Early on I learned to change everything quickly
The ground on which I walked, the air I was breathing
Lightly I do so, yet still I see
How others want to take too much with them.

Leave your ship light, leave lightly behind
Leave too your ship lightly behind when they tell you
To take the road inland.

You cannot be happy if you want to keep too much with you
Nor if you want what too many people do not want
Be wise, do not try to have your own way
But learn to grasp things as you pass by.
Leave your ship light, leave lightly behind
Leave too your ship lightly behind when they tell you
To take the road inland.

PLENTY TO SEE EVERYWHERE

What did you see, wanderer?
I saw a pleasant landscape; there was a grey hill against a clear
sky, and the grass waved in the wind. A house leaned
against the hill like a woman leaning against a man.
What did you see, wanderer?
I saw a ridge good to position guns behind.
What did you see, wanderer?
I saw a house so tumbledown that it had to be propped up by
a hill, which meant that it lay in shadow all day. I passed
it at various hours, and there was never smoke rising from
the chimney as if food were being cooked. And I saw people
who were living there.
What did you see, wanderer?
I saw a parched field on rocky ground. Each blade of grass
stood singly. Stones lay on the turf. A hill cast too much
shadow.
What did you see, wanderer?
I saw a rock raising its shoulder from the grassy soil like a
giant that refuses to be beaten. And the grass standing up stiff
and straight, proudly, on parched ground. And an indifferent
sky.
What did you see, wanderer?

I saw a fold in the ground. Thousands of years ago there
must have been great upheavals of the earth's surface here.
The granite lay exposed.
What did you see, wanderer?
No bench to sit on. I was tired.

INSTRUCT ME

When I was young I had a drawing made for me on a panel
With knife and wash, which showed an old chap
Scratching his chest because he is covered with scabs
Yet with a pleading look because he hopes to be instructed.
A second panel for the opposite corner of my room
Showing a young man instructing him
Was not finished.

When I was young I hoped
To find an old man prepared to have me instruct him.
When I am old I hope
A young man will find me, and I shall
Let myself be instructed.

VIII American Poems
1941–1947

ON THE SUICIDE OF THE REFUGEE W.B.

I'm told you raised your hand against yourself
Anticipating the butcher.
After eight years in exile, observing the rise of the enemy
Then at last, brought up against an impassable frontier
You passed, they say, a passable one.

Empires collapse. Gang leaders
Are strutting about like statesmen. The peoples
Can no longer be seen under all those armaments.

So the future lies in darkness and the forces of right
Are weak. All this was plain to you
When you destroyed a torturable body.

THE TYPHOON

On our flight from the house-painter to the States
We suddenly noticed that our little ship was not moving.
One whole night and one whole day
It lay against Luzon in the China Sea.
Some said it was because of a typhoon raging to the north
Others feared it was German raiders.
All
Preferred the typhoon to the Germans.

LANDSCAPE OF EXILE

But even I, on the last boat
Saw the gaiety of the dawn in the rigging
And the grayish bodies of dolphins emerge
From the Japanese Sea.

The little horsecarts with gilt decorations
And the pink sleeves of the matrons

In the alleys of doomed Manila
The fugitive beheld with joy.

The oil derricks and the thirsty gardens of Los Angeles
And the ravines of California at evening and the fruit market
Did not leave the messenger of misfortune unmoved.

AFTER THE DEATH OF MY COLLABORATOR M.S.

I
In Year Nine of the flight from Hitler
Exhausted by travelling
By cold and by hunger in wintry Finland
And by waiting for a passport to another continent
Our comrade Steffin died
In the red city of Moscow.

II
My general has fallen
My soldier has fallen

My pupil has gone away
My teacher has gone away

My nurse has gone
My nursling has gone.

III
Once the stage was reached where a not unkindly Death
Shrugged his shoulders and showed me her lungs' five
        ravaged lobes
Unable to imagine her surviving on the sixth alone
I rapidly assembled 500 jobs

Things that must be dealt with at once and tomorrow, next
    year
And in seven years' time from now
Asked endless questions, decisive ones
Unanswerable except by her
And thus needed
She died easier.

IV
In memory of my little teacher
Of her eyes, of the blue sparks of her anger
And of her old duffel coat with its deep hood
And deep bottom hem, I christened
Orion in the night sky the Steffin Constellation.
As I look up and observe it, shaking my head
I occasionally hear a feeble cough.

V
The wreckage

There is the wooden box still, holding slips for a play's
    construction
There are the Bavarian knives, there is the lectern for writing
    at
There is the blackboard, there are the masks still
There is the little radio and the military case
There is the answer, only there is no one to ask the questions
High above the garden
Stands the Steffin Constellation.

VI
After the death of my collaborator M.S.

Since you died, little teacher
I walk around restlessly, unseeing
In a grey world, stunned
As if laid off with nothing to occupy me.

No admission
To the workshop for me, or for
Any other stranger.

The roads and public gardens
I now see at unaccustomed hours, so that I
Hardly recognise them.

Home
I cannot go: I am ashamed
Of being laid off and
In misery.

SONNET IN EMIGRATION

Chased from my country now I have to see
If there's some shop or bar that I can find
Where I can sell the products of my mind.
Again I tread the roads well known to me

Worn smooth by those accustomed to defeat.
I'm on my way but don't yet know to whom.
Wherever I go they ask me: 'Spell your name!'
And oh, that name was once accounted great.

I should be glad now were it known to none
Like somebody for whom a warrant's out.
I hardly think they'd rush to take me on.

I dealt before with people such as these
And I suspect there may be growing doubt
Whether, in fact, my services would please.

ON THINKING ABOUT HELL

On thinking about Hell, I gather
My brother Shelley found it was a place
Much like the city of London. I
Who live in Los Angeles and not in London
Find, on thinking about Hell, that it must be
Still more like Los Angeles.

In Hell too
There are, I've no doubt, these luxuriant gardens
With flowers as big as trees, which of course wither
Unhesitantly if not nourished with very expensive water. And
        fruit markets
With great heaps of fruit, albeit having
Neither smell nor taste. And endless processions of cars
Lighter than their own shadows, faster than
Mad thoughts, gleaming vehicles in which
Jolly-looking people come from nowhere and are nowhere
        bound.
And houses, built for happy people, therefore standing empty
Even when lived in.

The houses in Hell, too, are not all ugly.
But the fear of being thrown on the street
Wears down the inhabitants of the villas no less than
The inhabitants of the shanty towns.

IN VIEW OF CONDITIONS IN THIS TOWN

In view of conditions in this town
This is how I act:

When I enter I give my name and show
Papers which prove it by stamps that
Cannot be forged.
When I say anything I cite witnesses of whose credibility
I have proofs.
When I say nothing I give my face
An expression of vacuity so it can be seen that
I am not thinking.
Thus
I allow no one to believe me. All forms of trust
I reject.

I do this because I know: conditions in this town
Make belief impossible.

Even so it sometimes happens –
I may be absent-minded or preoccupied –
That I am caught off guard and asked
If I am not a fraud, was not lying, was not
Keeping something back.
And I
Get more and more confused, I ramble and fail to mention
All that speaks in my favour; on the contrary
I am ashamed of myself.

CHILDREN'S CRUSADE

In 'thirty-nine in Poland
There was a bloody fight
And many a town and village
Turned to waste land overnight

Sisters lost their brothers
Wives were widowed by the war
And in fire and desolation
Children found their kin no more.

There came no news from Poland
Neither letter nor printed word
But in an eastern country
A curious tale is heard.

Snow fell, as they related
In a certain eastern town
How a new crusade of children
In Poland had begun.

For all along the highways
Troops of hungry children roamed
And gathered to them others
Who stood by ruined homes.

They wished to flee the slaughter
For the nightmare did not cease
And some day reach a country
Where there was peace.

They had a little leader
To show them where to go.
Yet he was sorely troubled
Since the way he did not know.

A girl of ten was carrying
A little child of four.
All she lacked to be a mother
Was a country without war.

In a coat with a velvet collar
A little Jew was dressed
He had been reared on whitest bread
But he marched on with the rest.

There was a thin and wretched boy
Who held himself apart.

That he came from a Nazi legation
Was a load of guilt in his heart.

They also had a dog with them
Which they had caught for food.
They spared it; so, another mouth
It followed where it would.

There was a school for penmanship
And teaching did not cease.
On the broken side of a tank
They learned to spell out *peace*.

A girl of twelve, a boy of fifteen
Had a love affair
And in a ruined farmyard
She sat and combed his hair.

But love could not endure
Cold wind began to blow:
And how can saplings bloom
When covered deep in snow?

They had a funeral besides
Two Poles and two Germans carried
The boy with the velvet collar
To the place where he was buried.

There were Catholics and Protestants
And Nazis at the grave
At the end a little Communist spoke
Of the future the living have.

So there was faith and hope
But lack of bread and meat.
And if they stole let no one blame
Who never bade them eat.

Let no one blame the poor man
Who never asked them in
For many have the will but have
No flour in the bin.

They strove to travel southward.
The south is where, 'tis said
At high noon the sun stands
Directly overhead.

They found a wounded soldier
In a pinewood one day.
And for a week they tended him
In hopes he'd know the way.

To Bilgoray, he said to them.
The fever made him rave.
Upon the eighth day he died.
They laid him in his grave.

Sometimes there were signposts
Though covered up in snow
All turned around and pointing wrong
But this they did not know.

And no grim joke it was, but done
On military grounds.
And long they sought for Bilgoray
Which never could be found.

They stood about their leader
Who stared at the snowy sky.
He pointed with his finger
Saying: Yonder it must lie.

Once, at night, they saw a fire
They turned away in fear.

Once three tanks came rolling by
Which meant that men were near.

Once, when they reached a city
They veered and went around.
They travelled then by night alone
Till they had passed the town.

Towards what was south-east Poland
In deeply drifting snow
The five and fifty children
Were last seen to go.

And if I close my eyes
I see them wander on
From one ruined barnyard
To another one.

Above them in the clouds I see
A new and greater host
Wearily breasting the cold wind
Homeless and lost

Seeking for a land of peace
Without the crash and flame of war
That scars the soil from which they came
And this host is always more.

Now in the gloom it seems to me
They come from many other places:
In the changing clouds I see
Spanish, French, yellow faces.

In January of that year
Poles caught a hungry dog
Around whose neck a placard hung
'Twas tied there with a cord.

These words thereon were: Please send help!
We don't know where we are.
We are five and fifty
The dog will lead you here.

And if you cannot come to us
Please drive him out.
Don't shoot the dog for no one else
Can find the spot.

A childish hand had written
The words the peasants read.
Since that time two years have passed.
The starving dog is dead.

TO THE GERMAN SOLDIERS IN THE EAST

1
Brothers, if I were with you –
Were one of you out there in the eastern snowfields
One of the thousands of you amid the iron chariots –
I would say as you say: Surely
There must be a road leading home.

But brothers, dear brothers
Under my steel helmet, under my skull
I would know what you know: There
Is no longer a road leading home.

On the map in a schoolboy's atlas
The road to Smolensk is no bigger
Than the Führer's little finger, but
In the snowfields it is further
Very far, too far.

The snow will not last for ever, just till springtime.
But men will not last for ever either. Springtime
Will be too long.

So I must die, I know it.
In the bandits' tunic I must die
Dying in the bloody arsonists' shirt.

As one of the many, one of the thousands
Hunted as bandits, slain as bloody arsonists.

2

Brothers, if I were with you
Were trudging with you across the icy wastes
I would ask as you ask: Why
Have I come here, whence
There is no longer any road leading home?

Why have I put on the bandits' tunic?
Why have I put on the bloody arsonists' shirt?
No, it was not from hunger
No, it was not from desire to kill.

Merely because I was a menial
And was ordered to
I set out to murder and to burn
And must now be hunted
And must now be slain.

3

Because I broke into
The peaceful land of peasants and workers
With its great order, its ceaseless construction
Trampling down crops and crushing down farmhouses
To plunder its workshops, its mills and its dams
To cut short the teaching in its thousand schools
To break up the sessions of its tireless committees:

Therefore I must now die like a rat
Caught by the farmer.

4

So that all trace of me may be wiped from
The face of the earth –
Of the leprosy that is me! That an example be made
Of me for all ages, how to deal
With bandits and bloody arsonists
And the menials of bandits and bloody arsonists.

5

So that mothers may say that they have no children.
So that children may say they have no fathers.
So that there may be mounds of earth which give no informa-
      tion.

6

And I shall never again see
The land from which I came
Not the Bavarian forests, nor the southern mountains
Not the sea, not the moors of Brandenburg, the pinetrees
Nor the Franconian vineyards sloping down to the river
Not in the grey dawn, not at midday
And not as evening falls.

Nor the cities, and the city where I was born.
Not the workbenches, nevermore the parlour
And not the chair.

All this I shall never again see
And no one who came with me
Will ever see it again.

Nor will I or you
Hear the voice of wives and mothers
Or the wind in the chimney in our homes
Or the cheerful sounds of the city, or the bitter.

7

No, I shall die in the prime of my life
Unloved, unmissed
A war device's reckless driver.

Untaught, save in my last hour
Untried, save in murdering
Not missed, save by the slaughterers.

And I shall lie under the earth
Which I have ravaged
A vandal without friends.
A sigh of relief will go up over my grave.

For what will they be burying?
A hundredweight of meat in a tank, soon to rot.
What will come of it?
A shrivelled bush, all frozen
A mess they shovelled away
A smell blown away by the wind.

8

Brothers, if I were now with you
On the road back to Smolensk
Back from Smolensk to nowhere

I would feel what you feel: From the start
I knew under my steel helmet, under my skull
That bad is not good
That two and two make four
And that all will die who went with him
The bloodstained bawler
The bloodstained fool.

Who did not know that the road to Moscow is long
Very long, too long.
That the winter in Eastern Europe is cold
Very cold, too cold.
That the peasants and workers of the new state would
Defend their earth and their cities
Till we are all blotted out.

9

By the forests, behind the guns
In the streets and in the houses
Between the tanks, by the roadside
At the hands of the men, of the women, of the children
In the cold, in the dark, in hunger

Till we are all blotted out
Today or tomorrow or the next day
You and me and the general, all
Who came here to lay waste
What men's hands had erected.

10

Because it is such hard work to cultivate the earth
Because it cost so much sweat to put up a house
To saw the beams, to draw the plan
To lay the walls, to cover the roof.
Because it was so exhausting, because the hopes were so high.

11

For a thousand years it was a matter for laughter
When the works of men's hands were violated.
But now the word will go round every continent:
The foot which trampled the new tractor drivers' fields
Has withered.
The hand which was raised against the new city builders'
        works
Has been hacked off.

SONG OF A GERMAN MOTHER

My son, your shiny boots and
Brown shirt were a present from me:
If I'd known then what I know now
I'd have hanged myself from a tree.

My son, when I saw your hand raised
In the Hitler salute that first day
I didn't know those who saluted
Would see their hand wither away.

My son, I can hear your voice speaking:
Of a race of heroes it tells.
I didn't know, guess or see that
You worked in their torture cells.

My son, when I saw you marching
In Hitler's victorious train
I didn't know he who marched off then
Would never come back again.

My son, you told me our country
Was about to come into its own.
I didn't know all it would come to
Was ashes and bloodstained stone.

I saw you wearing your brown shirt.
I should have protested aloud
For I did not know what I now know:
It was your burial shroud.

DELIVER THE GOODS

Again and again
As I walk through their cities
Seeking a living, I am told:
Show us what you're made of

Lay it on the table!
Deliver the goods!
Say something to inspire us!
Tell us of our own greatness!
Divine our secret desires!
Show us the way out
Make yourself useful!
Deliver the goods!

Stand alongside us, so that
You tower over us
Show that you are one of us.
We'll make you our hero.
We can pay too, we have the wherewithal –
No one else has.
Deliver the goods!

Know that our great showmen
Are those who show what we want to have shown.
Dominate by serving us!
Endure by winning duration for us
Play our game, we'll share the loot
Deliver the goods! Be straight with us!
Deliver the goods.

When I look into their decomposing faces
My hunger disappears.

SUMMER 1942

Day after day
I see the fig trees in the garden
The rosy faces of the dealers who buy lies
The chessmen on the corner table
And the newspapers with their reports
Of bloodbaths in the Soviet Union.

HOLLYWOOD ELEGIES

I

The village of Hollywood was planned according to the
      notion
People in these parts have of heaven. In these parts
They have come to the conclusion that God
Requiring a heaven and a hell, didn't need to
Plan two establishments but
Just the one: heaven. It
Serves the unprosperous, unsuccessful
As hell.

II

By the sea stand the oil derricks. Up the canyons
The gold prospectors' bones lie bleaching. Their sons
Built the dream factories of Hollywood.
The four cities
Are filled with the oily smell
Of films.

III

The city is named after the angels
And you meet angels on every hand.
They smell of oil and wear golden pessaries
And, with blue rings round their eyes
Feed the writers in their swimming pools every morning.

IV

Beneath the green pepper trees
The musicians play the whore, two by two
With the writers. Bach
Has written a Strumpet Voluntary. Dante wriggles
His shrivelled bottom.

V

The angels of Los Angeles
Are tired out with smiling. Desperately
Behind the fruit stalls of an evening
They buy little bottles
Containing sex odours.

VI

Above the four cities the fighter planes
Of the Defense Department circle at a great height
So that the stink of greed and poverty
Shall not reach them.

THE SWAMP

I saw many friends, and among them the friend I loved most
Helplessly sink into the swamp
I pass by daily.

And a drowning was not over
In a single morning. Often it took
Weeks; this made it more terrible.
And the memory of our long talks together
About the swamp, that already
Had claimed so many.

Helpless I watched him, leaning back
Covered with leeches
In the shimmering
Softly moving slime:
Upon the sinking face
The ghastly
Blissful smile.

HOLLYWOOD

Every day, to earn my daily bread
I go to the market where lies are bought
Hopefully
I take up my place among the sellers.

OF SPRINKLING THE GARDEN

O sprinkling the garden, to enliven the green!
Watering the thirsty trees. Give them more than enough
And do not forget the shrubs
Even those without berries, the exhausted
Niggardly ones. And do not neglect
The weeds growing between the flowers, they too
Are thirsty. Nor water only
The fresh grass or only the scorched.
Even the naked soil you must refresh.

READING THE PAPER WHILE BREWING THE TEA

In the early hours I read in the paper of epoch-making projects
On the part of pope and sovereigns, bankers and oil barons.
With my other eye I watch
The pot with the water for my tea
The way it clouds and starts to bubble and clears again
And overflowing the pot quenches the fire.

AND THE DARK TIMES NOW
CONTINUE

And the dark times now continue
In the other town
Yet the step is still a light one
The brow without a frown.

Hard humanity, uncaring
Like fishfolk long in ice
Yet the heart's still quick to answer
And a smile melts the face.

CALIFORNIAN AUTUMN

I
In my garden
Are nothing but evergreens. If I want to see autumn
I drive to my friend's country house in the hills. There
I can stand for five minutes and see a tree
Stripped of its foliage, and foliage stripped of its trunk.

II
I saw a big autumn leaf which the wind
Was driving along the road, and I thought: tricky
To reckon that leaf's future course.

THE MASK OF EVIL

On my wall hangs a Japanese carving
The mask of an evil demon, decorated with gold lacquer.
Sympathetically I observe
The swollen veins of the forehead, indicating
What a strain it is to be evil.

HOUNDED OUT BY SEVEN NATIONS

Hounded out by seven nations
Saw old idiocies performed:
Those I praise whose transmutations
Leave their persons undeformed.

E.P., L'ÉLECTION DE SON SÉPULCRE

The production of petrifactions
Is an arduous business and
Expensive. Whole towns
Must be reduced to rubble
And at times in vain
If the fly or the fern
Was badly placed. Furthermore
The stone of our towns is not lasting
And even petrifactions
Can't be relied on to last.

YOUNG MAN ON THE ESCALATOR

Son of the man the house was purchased by
When you ride down the stairs
He hoped as he came to die
That you'd fulfil his prayers.

Injure a foot, and it won't be
Easily healed again.
The ground was level which you see
Now split in twain.

Then as you place your foot and feel
The steps slide apart
Do you realise you're due to start
Shortly to rise or fall?

Step rises up, step drops away
Foot forward then? Foot back?
Do you think a failure may
Be healed by luck?

Right. That's the upper step you're trying.
But you'll observe: forgotten

Are the day's light, the voices crying.
Oh, the whole long stairway's streaming to the bottom.

And that is where you too are bound.
Do you get the plan?
You there on the stairway, son of the man
Who walked on level ground.

THE DEMOCRATIC JUDGE

In Los Angeles, before the judge who examines people
Trying to become citizens of the United States
Came an Italian restaurant keeper. After grave preparations
Hindered, though, by his ignorance of the new language
In the test he replied to the question:
What is the 8th Amendment? falteringly:
1492. Since the law demands that applicants know the
     language
He was refused. Returning
After three months spent on further studies
Yet hindered still by ignorance of the new language
He was confronted this time with the question: Who was
The victorious general in the Civil War? His answer was:
1492. (Given amiably, in a loud voice). Sent away again
And returning a third time, he answered
A third question: For how long a term are our Presidents
     elected?
Once more with: 1492. Now
The judge, who liked the man, realised that he could not
Learn the new language, asked him
How he earned his living and was told: by hard work. And so
At his fourth appearance the judge gave him the question:
When
Was America discovered? And on the strength of his correctly
     answering
1492, he was granted his citizenship.

NEW AGES

A new age does not begin all of a sudden.
My grandfather was already living in the new age
My grandson will probably still be living in the old one.

The new meat is eaten with the old forks.

It was not the first cars
Nor the tanks
It was not the airplanes over our roofs
Nor the bombers.

From new transmitters came the old stupidities.
Wisdom was passed on from mouth to mouth.

THE FISHING-TACKLE

In my room, on the whitewashed wall
Hangs a short bamboo stick bound with cord
With an iron hook designed
To snag fishing-nets from the water. The stick
Came from a second-hand store downtown. My son
Gave it to me for my birthday. It is worn.
In salt water the hook's rust has eaten through the binding.
These traces of use and of work
Lend great dignity to the stick. I
Like to think that this fishing-tackle
Was left behind by those Japanese fishermen
Whom they have now driven from the West Coast into camps
As suspect aliens; that it came into my hands
To keep me in mind of so many
Unsolved but not insoluble
Questions of humanity.

URBAN LANDSCAPE

1

You, forked out of the sardine tin
Individuals again, as intended by your mothers
Between cup and lip, once more
With an unusual eye, maybe a particular brow!
Glistening with the oil of reassurance and consolation
That keeps you fresh, pressed somewhat flat
With knife-edge creases, you accountants, it is you
I seek, the vaunted contents
Of the cities!

2

The water in the gutters
Is still panned for gold.
Vast in dismissal
Above the rooftops, the smoke
Takes itself off.

3

In the back yard hangs washing: a woman's
Pink pants, the wind
Climbs in.

4

The city sleeps. It swallows
Its sleep down hungrily. Gurgling
It lies in the gutter, haunted
By impure dreams and
Anxiety about the next meal.

5

The streams of humanity
Slop over the business districts
Which have been cleansed during the night
Of the dirt and devastation of the stream of humanity
Of the previous day.

6

Among the drab streams of humanity
That lap against the sides of the buildings
Float sheets of newspaper
Which swirl round monuments and
Climb up the office blocks.

7

The nine peoples of the city sleep
Exhausted
By their sins and the sins of others.
Their tools
Lie ready for the next day's work. Through the empty streets
Resound the steps of the watchmen.
At a remote airfield, laboriously
The bombers
Get off the ground.

CONTRADICTIONS

And a generation I saw with the skill to build themselves
        towers
High up into sunlight, as none before them, and living in
        caverns
Knowing how soil is nourished to yield them a twofold
        cropping.
But fed on the bark of trees and never found all that they
        needed.
And this was the place in the sky where the bomber squadrons
        above them
Murderously appeared and rose like the tides of the ocean
Only less punctually, for it was nature, but none understood
        it.
As once before it was the unpredictable weather
That determined drought and moisture, likewise the size of
        the harvests

Only not quite; for then returning in terrible cycles
Grain was shovelled into the fire, and beans into water.
And since much took place that no common man could
        provide for
In the shape of spells that moved mountains, diverted rivers
The gods re-emerged, the old gods, out of primordial
        darkness.

THE TRANSFORMATION OF THE GODS

The old heathen gods – this is a secret –
Were the earliest converts to Christianity.
Before the whole people they stepped through the grey ilex
        groves
Mumbled homely prayers and crossed themselves.

Throughout the entire middle ages they took their stand
As if absent-mindedly in the stone niches of God's house
Wherever godlike figures might be required.

And at the time of the French Revolution
They were the first to don the golden masks of pure reason
And as powerful concepts
They stepped, the old bloodsuckers and thought-stiflers
Across the bent backs of the toiling masses.

THE ACTIVE DISCONTENTED

The active discontented, your great teachers
Worked out the structure of a community
Where man is not a wolf to man
And discovered man's delight in eating his fill and having a
        roof over his head
And his wish to manage his own affairs.

They did not believe the preachers' babble
That our terrible hunger will be appeased once our bellies
     have rotted.
They chucked out the dishes full of bad food.
They recognised the man they were told was the enemy
As their hungry neighbour.
They were patient only in the struggle against the oppressors
Tolerant only of those who would not tolerate exploitation
Tired only of injustice.

He who kicked away the chair on which he sat uncomfortably
Who drove the ploughshare an inch deeper into the earth than
     any before him
The discontented man, he shall be our teacher
In reconstructing the community.

Those however
Who gorged themselves full on a plate of promises
Shall get their bellies ripped out.
Hiding their crooked bones
Is a waste of a spoonful of sand.

LETTERS ABOUT THINGS READ

    (Horace, Epistles II, i)

I
Take care, you
Who hymn Hitler! I
Who have seen the May and October processions
On the Red Square and the inscriptions
On their banners, and on the Pacific coast
On the Roosevelt Highway the thundering
Gasoline convoys and carriers laden
With five automobiles, one on top of the other, know

That soon he will die and dying
Will have outlived his fame, but even
If he were to succeed in making this earth
Uninhabitable, by
Conquering it, no song
In his honour could last. Too soon, admittedly
The scream of agony, a whole continent's even
Dies away to be able to stifle
The torturer's eulogy. True
Even those who hymn misdeeds may possess
Mellifluous voices. And yet
The dying swan's voice is counted the loveliest: he
Sings without fear.

In the little garden at Santa Monica
I read in the pepper tree's shade
I read in Horace of a certain Varius
Who hymned Augustus (that is, what good luck, his generals
And the Romans' corruption did for him). Only small
        fragments
Preserved in another man's work attest
Great poetic skill. It was not worth
The labour to copy more.

II
With pleasure I read
How Horace traced the Saturnian art of verse
Back to those peasant burlesques
Which did not spare great families, till
The police forbade lampoons, compelling
Those with a grudge to develop
An art more noble and air it
In lines more subtle. At least that is how
I construe that passage.

HOMECOMING

My native city, however shall I find her?
Following the swarms of bombers
I come home.
Well, where is she? Where the colossal
Mountains of smoke stand.
That thing there amongst the fires
Is her.

My native city, how will she receive me?
Before me go the bombers. Deadly swarms
Announce my homecoming to you. Conflagrations
Precede your son.

I, THE SURVIVOR

I know of course: it's simply luck
That I've survived so many friends. But last night in a dream
I heard those friends say of me: 'Survival of the fittest'
And I hated myself.

THE NEW VERONICA

When the big man came away bleeding
Guilty of having put up with it
Coming away from slavery and on his way to slavery
He was met by a fat fellow who shook his head and
Smelling slightly of Indian musk
Drew a sheet of paper from his swollen wallet
And handed it to the bleeding man before all the people
Then, in full view of the applauding people
Tolerantly wiped away the man's
Sweat, and the fat fellow
Took back the paper which now

Bore the image of the bleeding man's features
Waved it before the crowd
And sent it
To the Mint.

A FILM OF THE COMEDIAN CHAPLIN

Into a bistro on the Boulevard Saint-Michel
One rainy autumn night a young painter came
Drank three or four of those green spirits, and bored
The billiard players with the story of his stirring reunion
With a former mistress, a delicate creature
Now the wife of a wealthy butcher.
'Quick, gentlemen', he urged, 'please hand me the chalk
From your table', and kneeling on the floor
With a tremulous hand he tried to draw her picture
Her, the beloved of bygone days, despairingly
Rubbing out what he had drawn, beginning again
Stopping once more, combining
Other features and mumbling: 'Only yesterday I knew them'.
Cursing clients tripped over him, the angry landlord
Took hold of him by the collar and threw him out, but
Tireless on the pavement, shaking his head, with the chalk he
Chased after those fading features.

LAUGHTON'S BELLY

All of them, the way they carry their bellies around
You'd think it was swag with someone in pursuit of it
But the great man Laughton performed his like a poem
For his edification and nobody's discomfort.
Here it was: not unexpected, but not usual either
And built of foods which he
At his leisure had selected, for his entertainment.
And to a good plan, excellently carried out.

LIGHT AS THOUGH NEVER TOUCHING THE FLOOR

Light as though never touching the floor and obeying
Phantasmal drumming the two unfortunate princely brothers
Came on to the stage and duly began
To be there on the light-encircled boards. And the distances
Remained agreeable between the groups and whirring like
     knives
Infallible and quivering in the bull's-eye
The sentences came, but grouping and cadence
Hung between long memorised chance and half
Forgotten design. Quickly the guard was chosen
The spy engaged, the thinker hired and, pained
With frozen smiles, the Court heard the princely brothers
Exhort their sister urgently to be chaste, recommend
Virginity to the beautiful girl. Brief farewell. Refused
Is the embrace never offered. Alone
Stands the chaste one, abjuring
Chastity.

BURIAL OF THE ACTOR

When the changeable one had died
They laid him in the little whitewashed room
With a prospect of plants for the visitor
Put on the floor at his feet
Saddle and book, drink mixer and looking-glass
Hung on the wall the iron hook
For spiking scraps of paper recording
Unforgotten kindnesses on the dead man's part, and
Let the visitors in.

And in came his friends
(Also such of his relatives as were well disposed towards him)
His colleagues and his pupils, to hand in
The scraps of paper recording
Unforgotten kindnesses on the dead man's part.

When they bore the changeable one into his former house
Before him they bore the masks
Of his five great portrayals
Three of them classic and two controversial
But his covering was the red flag
Gift of the workers
For his unchangeableness in the days of oppression
And his achievements in the days of upheaval.

At the entrance, also, of his former house
The representatives of the Soviets read the text of his dismissal
With its description of his achievements, its erasure
Of all black marks and its warning to the living
To try to be like him and to fill up the gap he left.

Then they buried him in the public park, where the
Lovers' benches stand.

GARDEN IN PROGRESS

High above the Pacific coast, below it
The waves' gentle thunder and the rumble of oil tankers
Lies the actor's garden.

Giant eucalyptus trees shade the white house
Dusty relics of the former mission.
Nothing else recalls it, save perhaps the Indian
Granite snake's head that lies by the fountain
As if patiently waiting for
A number of civilisations to collapse.

And there was a Mexican sculpture of porous tufa
Set on a block of wood, portraying a child with malicious eyes
Which stood by the brick wall of the toolshed.

Lovely grey seat of Chinese design, facing
The toolshed. As you sit on it talking

You glance over your shoulder at the lemon hedge
With no effort.

The different parts repose or are suspended
In a secret equilibrium, yet never
Withdraw from the entranced gaze, nor does the masterly
    hand
Of the ever-present gardener allow complete uniformity
To any of the units: thus among the fuchsias
There may be a cactus. The seasons too
Continually order the view: first in one place then in another
The clumps flower and fade. A lifetime
Was too little to think all this up in. But
As the garden grew with the plan
So does the plan with the garden.

The powerful oak trees on the lordly lawn
Are plainly creatures of the imagination. Each year
The lord of the garden takes a sharp saw and
Shapes the branches anew.

Untended beyond the hedge, however, the grass runs riot
Around the vast tangle of wild roses. Zinnias and bright
    anemones
Hang over the slope. Ferns and scented broom
Shoot up around the chopped firewood.

In the corner under the fir trees
Against the wall you come on the fuchsias. Like immigrants
The lovely bushes stand unmindful of their origin
Amazing themselves with many a daring red
Their fuller blooms surrounding the small indigenous
Strong and delicate undergrowth of dwarf calycanthus.

There was also a garden within the garden
Under a Scotch fir, hence in the shade
Ten feet wide and twelve feet long

Which was as big as a park
With some moss and cyclamens
And two camelia bushes.

Nor did the lord of the garden take in only
His own plants and trees but also
The plants and trees of his neighbours; when told this
Smiling he admitted: I steal from all sides.
(But the bad things he hid
With his own plants and trees.)

Scattered around
Stood small bushes, one-night thoughts
Wherever one went, if one looked
One found living projects hidden.

Leading up to the house is a cloister-like alley of hibiscus
Planted so close that the walker
Has to bend them back, thus releasing
The full scent of their blooms.

In the cloister-like alley by the house, close to the lamp
Is planted the Arizona cactus, height of a man, which each
        year
Blooms for a single night, this year
To the thunder of guns from warships exercising
With white flowers as big as your fist and as delicate
As a Chinese actor.

Alas, the lovely garden, placed high above the coast
Is built on crumbling rock. Landslides
Drag parts of it into the depths without warning. Seemingly
There is not much time left in which to complete it.

IN FAVOUR OF A LONG, BROAD SKIRT

Your ample peasant skirt's the one to pick
Where cunningly I emphasise the length:
Lifting it off you to its full extent
Revealing thighs and bottom, gives a kick.
Then when you tuck your legs up on our sofa
Let it ride, so that, hidden in its shadow
Through deep discussions clouded in tobacco
Your flesh may hint our night is not yet over.

It is more than a base and lustful feeling
That makes me want a skirt as wide as this:
Your lovely movements bring to mind Colchis
The day Medea strolled towards the sea. –
These aren't the grounds, though, on which I'm appealing
For such a skirt. Base ones will do for me.

READING WITHOUT INNOCENCE

In his wartime journals
The writer Gide mentions a gigantic plane tree
He's been admiring – quite a while – for its enormous trunk
Its mighty branching and its equilibrium
Effected by the gravity of its preponderant boughs.

In far-off California
Shaking my head, I read this entry.
The nations are bleeding to death. No natural plan
Provides for a happy equilibrium.

ON HEARING THAT A MIGHTY STATESMAN HAS FALLEN ILL

If the indispensable man frowns
Two empires quake.

If the indispensable man dies
The world looks around like a mother without milk for her
      child.
If the indispensable man were to come back a week after his
      death
In the entire country there wouldn't be a job for him as a
      hall-porter.

THE OLD MAN OF DOWNING STREET

      'Sun, stand thou still upon Gibeon; and
      thou, Moon, in the valley of Ajalon.'

Tighten your leather belts, workmen of Flanders!
The old man of Downing Street breakfasts early today with
      the 300 men who betray you.
Bake your seed grain, peasants of the Campagna!
There will be no land. Neapolitan stevedores
On the walls of houses you will be daubing:
'Bring back the Stinker!' Today in the full light of noon
The old man of Downing Street was in Rome.

Keep your sons at home, mothers of Athens!
Or light candles for them: tonight
The old man of Downing Street is bringing back your King.

Get up from your beds, Labour peers!
Come and brush the old man of Downing Street's bloody coat!

ON THE NEWS OF THE TORY BLOOD BATHS
IN GREECE

Where the stench is biggest
The biggest words are spoken.
If a man has to stop his nose
How is he to stop his ears?

If the guns were not hoarse
They'd say: we do it for law and order.
If the butcher could spare the time
He'd say: my ends are unselfish.

After my compatriots, the classical scholars
Were driven from those Homeric fields
Where they researched into olive oil and cattle
The liberators returned from the war
To find new masters running the cities.

From between the guns the merchants crept out.

EVERYTHING CHANGES

Everything changes. You can make
A fresh start with your final breath.
But what has happened has happened. And the water
You once poured into the wine cannot be
Drained off again.

What has happened has happened. The water
You once poured into the wine cannot be
Drained off again, but
Everything changes. You can make
A fresh start with your final breath.

THE HINDMOST

The fight has been fought, let's eat!
Even the blackest times must come to an end.
Whatever was left after the fight should grasp its knife and
        fork.
The stronger man was he who survived
And the devil take the hindmost.

Get up, deadbeat!
The strong man is he who left no one behind.
Go out yet again, limp, crawl, lay about you
And bring in the hindmost!

WHAT HAS HAPPENED?

The industrialist is having his aeroplane serviced.
The priest is wondering what he said in his sermon eight
    weeks ago about tithes.
The generals are putting on civvies and looking like bank
    clerks.

Public officials are getting friendly.
The policeman points out the way to the man in the cloth
    cap.
The landlord comes to see whether the water supply is
    working.
The journalists write the word People with capital letters.
The singers sing at the opera for nothing.

Ships' captains check the food in the crew's galley.
Car owners get in beside their chauffeurs.
Doctors sue the insurance companies.
Scholars show their discoveries and hide their decorations.
Farmers deliver potatoes to the barracks.

The revolution has won its first battle:
That's what has happened.

NOW SHARE OUR VICTORY TOO

You shared our defeat, now share
Our victory too.

You warned us of many a wrong road
We walked it, you
Walked with us.

EPISTLE TO THE AUGSBURGERS

And then when it was the month of May
A Thousand-year Reich had passed away.

And down the street called Hindenburggass'
Came boys from Missouri with bazookas and cameras

Seeking the way, and what loot they could take
And one single German who thought World War II a
    mistake.

The Mis-Leader lay under the Chancellery
Of low-browed corpses with little moustaches there were two
    or three.

Field Marshals were rotting along the pavement
Butcher asked butcher to pass judgement.

The vetches flowered. The cocks were quietly moping.
The doors were closed. The roofs stood open.

PRIDE

When the American soldier told me
That the well fed middle class German girls
Could be bought for tobacco and the lower middle class
For chocolate
But the starved Russian slave workers could not be bought
I felt proud.

SWANSONG

Let the last inscription then run
(That broken slab without readers):

The planet is going to burst.
Those it bred will destroy it.

As a way of living together we merely thought up capitalism.
Thinking of physics, we thought up rather more:
A way of dying together.

WAR HAS BEEN GIVEN A BAD NAME

I am told that the best people have begun saying
How, from a moral point of view, the Second World War
Fell below the standard of the First. The Wehrmacht
Allegedly deplores the methods by which the SS effected
The extermination of certain peoples. The Ruhr industrialists
Are said to regret the bloody manhunts
Which filled their mines and factories with slave workers. The
          intellectuals
So I heard, condemn industry's demand for slave workers
Likewise their unfair treatment. Even the bishops
Dissociate themselves from this way of waging war; in short
          the feeling
Prevails in every quarter that the Nazis did the Fatherland
A lamentably bad turn, and that war
While in itself natural and necessary, has, thanks to the
Unduly uninhibited and positively inhuman
Way in which it was conducted on this occasion, been
Discredited for some time to come.

GERMANY 1945

Indoors is death by plague
Outdoors is death by cold.
So where are we to be?
The sow has shat in her bed
The sow's my mum. I said:
O mother mine, o mother mine
What have you done to me?

THE LOVELY FORK

When the fork with the lovely horn handle broke
It struck me that deep within it
There must always have been a fault. With difficulty
I summoned back to my memory
My joy in its flawlessness.

ONCE

This coldness once seemed wonderful to me
And the freshness brushed life into my skin
And the bitterness tasted good, and I felt free
To dine or not according to my whim
Supposing darkness were to ask me in.

Cold was the well from which I drew my vigour
And nothingness gave me this unbounded space.
Marvellous it was when a rare brilliant flicker
Cut through the natural darkness. Short-lived? Yes.
But I, old enemy, was always quicker.

EPITAPH FOR M.

The sharks I dodged
The tigers I slew
What ate me up
Was the bedbugs.

LETTER TO THE ACTOR CHARLES LAUGHTON
CONCERNING THE WORK ON THE PLAY 'THE LIFE
OF GALILEO'

Still your people and mine were tearing each other to pieces
        when we
Pored over those tattered exercise books, looking
Up words in dictionaries, and time after time
Crossed out our texts and then
Under the crossings-out excavated
The original turns of phrase. Bit by bit –
While the housefronts crashed down in our capitals –
The façades of language gave way. Between us
We began following what characters and actions dictated:
New text.

Again and again I turned actor, demonstrating
A character's gestures and tone of voice, and you
Turned writer. Yet neither I nor you
Stepped outside his profession.

ix Poems of Reconstruction
1947–1953

THE ANACHRONISTIC PROCESSION
OR
FREEDOM AND DEMOCRACY

Spring returned to Germany.
In the ruins you could see
Early green birch buds unfold
Graceful, tentative and bold

As from many a southern valley
Voters left their houses to rally
Forming a disjointed column
Underneath two banners solemn

Whose supports were all worm-eaten
Their inscription weatherbeaten
Though its gist appeared to be
Freedom and Democracy.

Every church bell started ringing.
Soldiers' widows, airmen's women
Orphaned, shell-shocked, crippled, raped
Open-mouthed the watchers gaped.

And the deaf could tell the blind
Who it was that marched behind
Such a slogan as, maybe
Freedom and Democracy.

At the head a featherbrain
Sang with all his might and main:
'Allons, enfants, God save the King
And the dollar, Kling, Kling, Kling.'

Next, with monstrance held up high
Two in monkish garb strode by.
As for what they wore below –
Did I glimpse a jack-boot's toe?

On their flag the cross looked thicker
Than the previous swastika.
Now the latter was outdated
It had been obliterated.

Under this there marched a father
Sent from Rome, where (so we gather)
He had left His Holiness
Gazing East in deep distress.

Next to celebrate the Night
Of the Long Knives, comes a tight
Knot of men who loudly call
For another free-for-all.

Then the faceless trust directors
Those men's patrons and protectors:
Pray, for our arms industry
Freedom and Democracy!

Like a cock worn out with rutting
A Pan-German passes, strutting
He wants Freedom of the Word (the
Word being 'Murder').

Keeping step, next march the teachers
Toadying, brain-corrupting creatures
For the right to educate
Boys to butchery and hate.

Then the medical advisers
Hitler's slaves, mankind's despisers
Asking, might they now select
A few Reds to vivisect.

Three grim dons, whose reputation
Rests on mass extermination

Stake their claim for chemistry:
Freedom and Democracy.

Next our whitewashed Nazi friends
On whom the new State depends:
Body lice, whose pet preserve is
In the higher civil service.

After them behold the former
Editors of Streicher's *Stürmer*
All set to protest unless
We get Freedom of the Press.

Next in line, honest taxpayers
Once renowned as semite-slayers
Gagged today, want guarantees
For the new minorities.

As for those parliamentarians
Who in Hitler's day were Aryans
And now pose as barristers:
Freedom for such gifts as theirs!

While the black market man, asked
Why he came out on the march
Unconditionally replies:
To preserve free enterprise.

And the judge (now this is rich)
Wields outmoded laws by which
Hitlerised up to the hilt, he
Finds men like himself not guilty.

Poets, painters and musicians
Seeking grub and good positions
Noble souls, who now assure us
They were no friends of the Führer's.

Through the streets resounds the lash:
SS men flogging for cash.
Freedom needs them too, you see –
Freedom and Democracy.

And those Nazi women there
With their skirts up in the air –
Legs, they reckon, are what gets
Allied sweets and cigarettes.

Strength-through-joy dames, spies, Jew-baiters
Gestapo investigators
Tax-gifts-interest stimulators
Irredentist liberators

Blood and dirt, elective allies
Winding over hills and valleys
Belched, stank, squittered out their plea:
Freedom and Democracy!

Till, all stinking fit to burst
They arrived in Munich, first
City of the Nazi Movement
Home of German self-entombment.

Misinformed, in misery
See its baffled bourgeoisie
Standing where their houses stood
Lacking certainties and food.

As the smelly column staggers
Through the rubble with its banners
By the Brown House there's a surge
And six silent shades emerge.

All now halt to mark this meeting
And the six, heads bared in greeting

Join the column which once more
Bears its banners on before.

In six cars those six assorted
Party members are transported
While the crowd shouts: Now we'll see
Freedom and Democracy.

Bony hand grasping a whip
First OPPRESSION takes a trip
In a half-track furnished free
By our heavy industry.

In a rusty tank, much greeted
Next comes PLAGUE. His breath is foetid.
To conceal his flaking skin
He wraps a brown scarf round his chin.

After him see FRAUD appear
Brandishing a jug of beer.
You will get your glasses filled when
You have let him take your children.

Older than the hills, and yet
Still out for what she can get
STUPIDITY staggers on board
Riveted she stares at Fraud.

Lolling back, as at a play
MURDER too is on his way
Perfectly at ease as he
Hums: Sweet dream of liberty.

Shaken by the latest crises
ROBBERY materialises
In Field-Marshal's uniform
With the globe beneath his arm.

Each of these six grisly figures
Firmly based, with ready triggers
Says that there has got to be
Freedom and Democracy.

Lurching, a huge hearse comes last
Once those six monsters have passed
Inside which, unseen and wretched
Who can tell what race lies stretched?

Cold winds blow a requiem
From the ruins over them
Former tenants of the flats
That once stood here. Then great rats

Leave the rubble in their masses
Join the column as it passes
Squeaking 'Freedom!' as they flee
'Freedom and Democracy!'

ANTIGONE

Emerge from the darkness and go
Before us a while
Friendly one, with the light step
Of total certainty, a terror
To wielders of terror.

You turn your face away. I know
How much you dreaded death, and yet
Even more you dreaded
Life without dignity.

And you would not let the mighty
Get away with it, nor would you

Compromise with the confusers, or ever
Forget dishonour. And over their atrocities
There grew no grass.

THE FRIENDS

The war separated
Me, the writer of plays, from my friend the stage designer.
The cities where we worked are no longer there.
When I walk through the cities that still are
At times I say: that blue piece of washing
My friend would have placed it better.

FOR HELENE WEIGEL

And now step in your easy way
On to the old stage in our demolished city
Full of patience, at the same time relentless
Showing what is right.

What is foolish, with wisdom
Hatred, with friendliness
Where the house has collapsed
What was wrong with the plans.

But to the unteachable now show
With some slight hope
Your good face.

OBSERVATION

When I returned
My hair was not yet grey
And I was glad

The travails of the mountains lie behind us.
Before us lie the travails of the plains.

A NEW HOUSE

Back in my country after fifteen years of exile
I have moved into a fine house.
Here I have hung
My Nō masks and picture scroll representing the Doubter.
Every day, as I drive through the ruins, I am reminded
Of the privileges to which I owe this house. I hope
It will not make me patient with the holes
In which so many thousands huddle. Even now
On top of the cupboard containing my manuscripts
My suitcase lies.

BAD TIMES

The tree tells why it bore no fruit.
The poet tells why his lines went wrong.
The general tells why the war was lost.

Pictures, painted on brittle canvas.
Records of exploration, handed down to the forgetful.
Great behaviour, observed by no one.

Should the cracked vase be used as a pisspot?
Should the ridiculous tragedy be turned into a farce?
Should the disfigured sweetheart be put in the kitchen?

All praise to those who leave crumbling houses.
All praise to those who bar their door against a demoralised
        friend.
All praise to those who forget about the unworkable plan.

The house is built of the stones that were available.
The rebellion was raised using the rebels that were available.
The picture was painted using the colours that were available.

Meals were made of whatever food could be had.
Gifts were given to the needy.
Words were spoken to those who were present.
Work was done with the existing resources, wisdom and
    courage.

Carelessness should not be forgiven.
More would have been possible.
Regret is expressed.
(What good could it do?)

TO MY COUNTRYMEN

You who survive in cities that have died
Now show some mercy to yourselves at last.
Don't march, poor things, to war as in the past
As if past wars left you unsatisfied.
I beg you – mercy for yourselves at last.

You men, reach for the spade and not the knife.
You'd sit in safety under roofs today
Had you not used the knife to make your way
And under roofs one leads a better life.
I beg you, take the spade and not the knife.

You children, to be spared another war
You must speak out and tell your parents plain.
You will not live in ruins once again
Nor undergo what they've had to endure.
You children, to be spared another war.

You mothers, since the word is yours to give
To stand for war or not to stand for war
I beg you, choose to let your children live.
Let birth, not death, be what they thank you for.
You mothers, choose to let your children live.

TO THE ACTOR P.L. IN EXILE

Listen, we are calling you back. Driven out
You must now return. The country
Out of which you were driven flowed once
With milk and honey. You are being called back
To a country that has been destroyed.
And we have nothing more
To offer you than the fact that you are needed.

Poor or rich
Sick or healthy
Forget everything
And come.

OBITUARY FOR XX

Speak of the weather
Be thankful he's dead
Who before he had spoken
Took back what he said.

ENCOUNTER WITH THE POET
AUDEN

Lunching me, a kindly act
In an alehouse, still intact
He sat looming like a cloud
Over the beer-sodden crowd.

And kept harping with persistence
On the bare fact of existence
I.e., a theory built around it
Recently in France propounded.

THE JOY OF GIVING

It surely is life's greatest joy
To give to those whose lot is hard
And with glad hands, impulsively
To scatter splendid gifts abroad.

What rose is fairer than the face
Of one to whom we play the donors?
Behold his hands, o highest bliss
Encumbered with our gracious favours.

Nothing can give so keen a pleasure
As helping each and every one.
What I possess I cannot treasure
Without a mind to pass it on.

Five Children's Songs, 1950

THE STORY OF MOTHER COURAGE

There once was a mother
Mother Courage they called her
In the Thirty Years' War
She sold victuals to soldiers.

The war did not scare her
From making her cut
Her three children went with her
And so got their bit.

Her first son died a hero
The second an honest lad
A bullet found her daughter
Whose heart was too good.

THE WARLIKE SCHOOLMASTER

There was a teacher called Huber.
He was all for war, for war.
When he spoke of old Fred the Great
You'd see his eye scintillate
But at President Pieck's name – never.

Along came washerwoman Schmitten
She was against dirt, against dirt.
She gave teacher Huber a shove
Right into the laundry tub
And washed him away just like that.

SUPERSTITION

Liza found four-leaved clover
Growing in the hedge.
Eager to fetch
It, jumping the ditch
She broke her favourite leg.

Spider in the morning
Liza's cheeks grew warm.
The day brought no disaster
And at bedtime Father
Brought raspberry ice cream.

The stork does not bring babies.
Seven does not bring luck.
And there is not any devil
In our Republic.

LITTLE SONG FROM OLDEN
TIMES

(NO LONGER TO BE SUNG
NOW)

One. Two. Three. Four.
Dad needs one pint more.
Four. Three. Two. One.
Mum don't need none.

LITTLE POSTWAR SONG

Spin, little top!
Our road's no longer up.
And Dad has got a house to fix
And Mum is picking out the bricks.
Spin, little top!

Fly, little kite!
Our sky is clear and bright.
So up you go and break your string
Fly over Moscow to Peking.
Fly, little kite!

CHILDREN'S ANTHEM

Spare no charm and spare no passion
Labour or intelligence
That a decent German nation
Flourish as do other lands.

That the people give up flinching
At the crimes which we evoke
And hold out their hand in friendship
As they do to other folk.

Neither over nor yet under
Other peoples will we be
From the Oder to the Rhineland
From the Alps to the North Sea.

And because we'll make it better
Let us guard and love our home
Love it as our dearest country
As the others love their own.

WHEN IT'S A NOTION

When it's a notion
When it's still vague
It is praised.
When it looms big
When plans are in motion
Objections are raised.

Six Late Theatre Poems

LOOKING FOR THE NEW AND OLD

When you read your parts
Exploring, ready to be surprised
Look for the new and old. For our time
And the time of our children is the time of struggles
Between the new and the old.
The cunning of the old working woman
Who relieves the teacher of his knowledge
Like a pack too heavy to carry, is new
And must be shown as new. And old
Is the fear of the workers in wartime
Reluctant to take the leaflets which will teach them; it must
Be shown as old. But
As the people say, at the moon's change of phases
The new moon for one night
Holds the old moon in its arms. The hesitancy of the timid
Proclaims the new time. Always
Fix the 'still' and the 'already'.
The struggles between the classes
The struggles between new and old
Rage also within each man.
The teacher's willingness to teach
Is overlooked by his brother, but the stranger
Sees it.
Check over all the feelings and actions of your characters
For new and old features.
The hopes of the trader Courage
Are mortal to her children; yet the dumb girl's
Despair about the war
Belongs with the new. Her helpless movements
As she drags her life-saving drum on to the roof
A great helper, should fill you

With pride; the energy
Of the trader who learns nothing, with compassion.
Reading your parts
Exploring, ready to be surprised
Rejoice at the new, be ashamed at the old!

THE CURTAINS

On the big curtain paint the cantankerous
Peace dove of my brother Picasso. Behind it
Stretch the wire rope and hang
My lightly fluttering half curtains
Which cross like two waves of foam to make
The working woman handing out pamphlets
And the recanting Galileo both disappear.
Following the change of plays they can be
Of rough linen or of silk
Or of white leather or of red, and so on.
Only don't make them too dark, for on them
You must project the titles of the following
Incidents, for the sake of tension and that
The right thing may be expected. And please make
My curtain half-height, don't block the stage off.
Leaning back, let the spectator
Notice the busy preparations being so
Ingeniously made for him, a tin moon is
Seen swinging down, a shingle roof
Is carried in; don't show him too much
But show something. And let him observe
That this is not magic but
Work, my friends.

THE LIGHTING

Give us some light on the stage, electrician. How can we
Playwrights and actors put forward
Our images of the world in half darkness? The dim twilight
Induces sleep. But we need the audience's
Wakeful-, even watchfulness. Let them
Do their dreaming in the light. The little bit of night
We now and then require can be
Indicated by moons or lamps, likewise our acting
Can make clear what time of day it is
Whenever needed. The Elizabethan wrote us verses
About a heath at evening
Which no electrician can match, nor even
The heath itself. So light up
What we have laboured over, that the audience
Can see how the outraged peasant woman
Sits down on the Finnish soil
As if it belonged to her.

THE SONGS

Separate the songs from the rest!
By some symbol of music, by change of lighting
By titles, by pictures now show
That the sister art is
Coming on stage. The actors
Change into singers. They have a new attitude
As they address themselves to the audience, still
Characters in the play but now also undisguisedly
Accomplices of the playwright.
Nanna Callas, the round-headed landlord's daughter
Brought to market like a hen
Sings the song of the mere
Change of masters, not to be understood without the wriggle
        of the hips

Trick of the trade that
Turned her privates into a scar. Not to be understood either
The canteen woman's song of the Great Capitulation, unless
The anger of the playwright
Is added to that of the woman.
But dry Ivan Vesovchikoff, the Bolshevik worker, sings
With the iron voice of the class that cannot be beaten
And friendly Vlassova, the mother
Reports, singing in her particular careful voice
That the banner of reason is red.

WEIGEL'S PROPS

Just as the millet farmer picks out for his trial plot
The heaviest seeds and the poet
The exact words for his verse so
She selects the objects to accompany
Her characters across the stage. The pewter spoon
Which Courage sticks
In the lapel of her Mongolian jacket, the party card
For warm-hearted Vlassova and the fishing net
For the other, Spanish mother or the bronze bowl
For dust-gathering Antigone. Impossible to confuse
The split bag which the working woman carries
For her son's leaflets, with the moneybag
Of the keen tradeswoman. Each item
In her stock is hand picked: straps and belts
Pewter boxes and ammunition pouches; hand picked too
The chicken and the stick which at the end
The old woman twists through the draw-rope
The Basque woman's board on which she bakes her bread
And the Greek woman's board of shame, strapped to her back
With holes for her hands to stick through, the Russian's
Jar of lard, so small in the policeman's hand; all
Selected for age, function and beauty
By the eyes of the knowing

The hands of the bread-baking, net-weaving
Soup-cooking connoisseur
Of reality.

ON SERIOUSNESS IN ART

The seriousness of the man who shapes the silver ornaments
Is likewise welcome in the art of the theatre, and welcome
Is the seriousness of people discussing the text
Of a pamphlet behind locked doors. But the seriousness
Of a doctor stooping over his patient is no longer compatible
With the art of the theatre, and it utterly bars
The seriousness of the priest, whether gentle or hectic.

THE MASTERS BUY CHEAP

The decors and costumes of the great Neher
Are made of cheap material
Out of wood, rags and colour
He makes the Basque fisherman's hovel
And imperial Rome.

So my woman friend out of a smile
Which she gets for nothing in the fish market
And gives away like the scales of fish
When she wants to, makes an event
That would have bribed Lao-tse.

LOVE SONGS

I
After I had gone from you
That ever-present day
And once again began to see
All that I saw were gay.

Since we passed that evening hour
You know the one I mean
My legs are nimbler by far
My mouth is more serene.

And since I felt so, tree and bush
And meadow grow more greenly
The very water when I wash
Flows over me more coolly.

II

Song of a Loving Woman

When you delight me
Then I think sometimes:
If I could die now
I would be happy
Till my life's end.

Then when you are old
And you think of me
I shall look as now
You'll have a sweetheart
That is still young.

III

Seven roses on the bush
Six belong to the wind
One will stay there, so there's just
One for me to find.

Seven times I'll summon you
Six times stay away
But the seventh, promise me
Come without delay.

IV

My dearest one gave me a branch
The leaves on it are brown.

The year is drawing to its close
Our love is just begun.

GOING DOWN EARLY TO THE VOID

Going down early to the void
Up from the void I'm filled anew.
When with nothingness I've stayed
I again know what to do.

When I love, or when I feel
Then it's just a further drain.
But I plunge into the cool
And am hot again.

ON A CHINESE CARVING OF A LION

The bad fear your claws.
The good enjoy your elegance.
This
I would like to hear said
Of my verse.

HAPPY ENCOUNTER

On Sundays in June among the saplings
Villagers looking for raspberries hear
Studious girls and women from the technical college
Pick out phrases from their textbooks
About dialectics and the care of children.

Looking up from their textbooks
The students see the villagers
Pick berries from the canes.

THE VOICE OF THE OCTOBER STORM

The voice of the October storm
Around the little house by the reeds
Strikes me as quite like my voice.
Comfortably
I lie on my bed and hear
Above the lake and above the city
My voice.

THE MAN WHO TOOK ME IN

The man who took me in
Lost his house.
The one who played for me
Had his instrument taken away.

Is he going to say
I bring death
Or: those who took everything from him
Bring death?

GERMANY 1952

O Germany, so torn in pieces
And never left alone!
The cold and dark increases
While each sees to his own.
Such lovely fields you'd have
Such cities thronged and gay;
If you'd but trust yourself
All would be child's play.

x Last Poems
1953–1956

THE BREAD OF THE PEOPLE

Justice is the bread of the people.
Sometimes it is plentiful, sometimes it is scarce.
Sometimes it tastes good, sometimes it tastes bad.
When the bread is scarce, there is hunger.
When the bread is bad, there is discontent.

Throw away the bad justice
Baked without love, kneaded without knowledge!
Justice without flavour, with a grey crust
The stale justice which comes too late!

If the bread is good and plentiful
The rest of the meal can be excused.
One cannot have plenty of everything all at once.
Nourished by the bread of justice
The work can be achieved
From which plenty comes.

As daily bread is necessary
So is daily justice.
It is even necessary several times a day.

From morning till night, at work, enjoying oneself.
At work which is an enjoyment.
In hard times and in happy times
The people requires the plentiful, wholesome
Daily bread of justice.

Since the bread of justice, then, is so important
Who, friends, shall bake it?

Who bakes the other bread?

Like the other bread
The bread of justice must be baked
By the people.

Plentiful, wholesome, daily.

LISTEN WHILE YOU SPEAK!

Don't say you are right too often, teacher.
Let the students realise it.
Don't push the truth:
It's not good for it.
Listen while you speak!

UNIDENTIFIABLE ERRORS OF THE ARTS
COMMISSION

Invited to a session of the Academy of Arts
The highest officials of the Arts Commission
Paid their tribute to the noble custom of
Accusing oneself of certain errors, and
Muttered that they too accused themselves
Of certain errors. Asked
What errors, however, they found it wholly impossible to
    recall
Any specific errors. Everything that
The Academy held against them had been
Precisely no error, for the Arts Commission
Had suppressed only worthless stuff, indeed had not
Suppressed it exactly, had just not pushed it.
Despite the most earnest ruminations
They could recall no specific errors, nonetheless
They were most insistent that they had
Committed errors – as is the custom.

THE OFFICE FOR LITERATURE

The Office for Literature is known to allot
Paper to the republic's publishing houses, so many hundred-
    weight
Of this precious substance for such works as are welcome.

Welcome
Are works with ideas
Familiar to the Office for Literature from the newspapers.
This custom
Given the sort of newspapers we've got
Should lead to great savings in paper, so long as
The Office for Literature confines itself to licensing one book
For each idea in the newspapers. Unfortunately
It allows virtually all those books to be printed which take an
      idea
From the newspapers and doctor it.
Hence
For the works of various masters
There is no paper.

NOT WHAT WAS MEANT

When the Academy of Arts demanded freedom
Of artistic expression from narrow-minded bureaucrats
There was a howl and a clamour in its immediate vicinity
But roaring above everything
Came a deafening thunder of applause
From beyond the Sector boundary.

Freedom! it roared. Freedom for the artists!
Freedom all round! Freedom for all!
Freedom for the exploiters! Freedom for the warmongers!
Freedom for the Ruhr cartels! Freedom for Hitler's generals!
Softly, my dear fellows . . .

The Judas kiss for the artists follows
Hard on the Judas kiss for the workers.
The arsonist with his bottle of petrol
Sneaks up grinning to
The Academy of Arts.

But it was not to embrace him, just
To knock the bottle out of his dirty hand that
We asked for elbow room.
Even the narrowest minds
In which peace is harboured
Are more welcome to the arts than the art lover
Who is also a lover of the art of war.

Buckow Elegies

MOTTO

Were a wind to arise
I could put up a sail
Were there no sail
I'd make one of canvas and sticks.

CHANGING THE WHEEL

I sit by the roadside
The driver changes the wheel.
I do not like the place I have come from.
I do not like the place I am going to.
Why with impatience do I
Watch him changing the wheel?

THE FLOWER GARDEN

By the lake, deep amid fir and silver poplar
Sheltered by wall and hedge, a garden
So wisely plotted with monthly flowers
That it blooms from March until October.

Here, in the morning, not too frequently, I sit
And wish I too might always
In all weathers, good or bad
Show one pleasant aspect or another.

THE SOLUTION

After the uprising of the 17th June
The Secretary of the Writers' Union
Had leaflets distributed in the Stalinallee
Stating that the people
Had forfeited the confidence of the government
And could win it back only
By redoubled efforts. Would it not be easier
In that case for the government
To dissolve the people
And elect another?

GREAT TIMES, WASTED

I knew that cities were being built
I haven't been to any.
A matter for statistics, I thought
Not history.

What's the point of cities, built
Without the people's wisdom?

NASTY MORNING

The silver poplar, a celebrated local beauty
Today an old harridan. The lake
A puddle of dish-water, don't touch!
The fuchsias amongst the snapdragon cheap and vain.
Why?
Last night in a dream I saw fingers pointing at me
As at a leper. They were worn with toil and
They were broken.

You don't know! I shrieked
Conscience-stricken.

STILL AT IT

The plates are slammed down so hard
The soup slops over.
In shrill tones
Resounds the order: Now eat!

The Prussian eagle
Jabbing food down
The gullets of its young.

HOT DAY

Hot day. My writing-case on my knee
I sit in the summer-house. A green boat
Appears through the willow. In the stern
A stout nun, stoutly clad. In front of her
An elderly person in a bathing-costume, probably a priest.
At the oars, rowing for all he's worth
A child. Just like old times, I think
Just like old times.

THE TRUTH UNITES

Friends, I'd like you to know the truth and speak it.
Not like tired, evasive Caesars: 'Tomorrow grain will come.'
But like Lenin: By tomorrow
We'll be done for, unless . . .
As the jingle has it:
 'Brothers, my first obligation
 Is to tell you outright:
 We're in a tough situation
 With no hope in sight.'
Friends, a wholehearted admission
And a wholehearted UNLESS!

THE SMOKE

The little house among trees by the lake.
From the roof smoke rises.
Without it
How dreary would be
House, trees and lake.

IRON

In a dream last night
I saw a mighty storm.
It clutched the scaffolding
It ripped down the builders' ladders
Made of iron.
But all that was of wood
Gave and held.

FIRS

In the early hours
The fir-trees are copper.
That's how I saw them
Half a century ago
Two world wars ago
With young eyes.

THE ONE-ARMED MAN IN THE UNDERGROWTH

Dripping with sweat he bends down
To gather brushwood. The mosquitoes
He fends off with shakes of the head. Between his knees
He laboriously bundles his firewood. Groaning

He straightens himself, holds up his hand to feel
If it's raining. Hand upraised
The dreaded S.S. man.

EIGHT YEARS AGO

There was a time
When all was different here.
The butcher's wife knows.
The postman has too erect a gait.
And what was the electrician?

PADDLING, TALKING

It's evening. Two canoes
Glide past, inside them
Two naked young men: paddling abreast
They talk. Talking
They paddle abreast.

READING HORACE

Even the Flood
Did not last for ever.
There came a time
When the black waters ebbed.
Yes, but how few
Have lasted longer.

SOUNDS

Later, in autumn
The silver poplars harbour great swarms of rooks

But all summer long when
The region is birdless I hear
Only sounds of human origin.
I have no objection.

READING A SOVIET BOOK

To tame the Volga, I read
Will not be an easy task. She will call
On her daughters for help, on the Oka, Kama, Unsha,
        Vyetluga
And her granddaughters, the Chussovaya, the Vyatka.
She'll summon all her forces, with waters from seven thousand
        tributaries
Full of rage she'll crash down on the Stalingrad dam.
That genius of invention, with the devilish cunning
Of the Greek Odysseus, will make use of every fissure
Deploy on the right flank, by-pass on the left, take cover
Underground – but, I read, the Soviet people
Who love her, sing songs about her, have recently
Studied her and no later
Than 1958
Will tame her.
And the black fields of the Caspian plains
The arid, the stepchildren
Will reward them with bread.

THIS SUMMER'S SKY

High above the lake a bomber flies.
From the rowing boats
Children look up, women, an old man. From a distance
They appear like young starlings, their beaks
Wide open for food.

THE TROWEL

In a dream I stood on a building site. I was
A bricklayer. In my hand
I held a trowel. But when I bent down
For mortar, a shot rang out
That tore half the iron
Off my trowel.

THE MUSES

When the man of iron beats them
The Muses sing louder.
With blackened eyes
They adore him like bitches.
Their buttocks twitch with pain.
Their thighs with lust.

READING A LATE GREEK POET

At the time when their fall was certain –
On the ramparts the lament for the dead had begun –
The Trojans adjusted small pieces, small pieces
In the triple wooden gates, small pieces.
And began to take courage, to hope.

The Trojans too, then.

ON THE BERLINER ENSEMBLE'S MOVE TO THE
THEATER AM SCHIFFBAUERDAMM

At first you acted in the ruins. Now
You'll act in this fine house, for something more than fun.
From you and us a peaceful WE must grow
To help this house to last, and many another one.

TO A WOMAN COLLEAGUE WHO STAYED BEHIND IN
THE THEATRE DURING THE SUMMER VACATION

Across the courtyard I see you go into the dramaturgs'
Building and, up the stairs, to the hall where
Under our comrade Picasso's poster, in blue tobacco smoke
Plays are cast and texts are cut and new rehearsals
Are fixed, while the telephone
Forever rings, regardless. I follow you
On to the photographer's rooms and see you
Fetch pictures for France and again
I cross the courtyard with you and look at the stage
Where builders now must be getting rid of those troublesome
        corners
To make room for the new cyclorama for
Coriolanus and dropping dust on the place where
The chair of Azdak stands.

1954: FIRST HALF

No serious sickness, no serious enemies.
Enough work.
And I got my share of the new potatoes
The cucumbers, asparagus, strawberries.
I saw the lilac in Buckow, the market square in Bruges
The canals of Amsterdam, the Halles in Paris.

I enjoyed the kindness of delightful A.T.
I read Voltaire's letters and Mao's essay on contradiction.
I put on the Chalk Circle at the Berliner Ensemble.

ONLY A FLEETING
GLANCE

'Only a fleeting glance
Could take her in
So it was merely chance
Made me her man.'

> 'Only in passing I
> Entered his life
> So, unregardedly
> Became his wife.'

Both let the time go by
Till it was spent
Put on our overcoats
Embraced, and went.

THE LITTLE ROSE, OH HOW SHOULD IT
BE LISTED?

The little rose, oh how should it be listed?
Suddenly dark red and young and near?
Oh we never knew that it existed
Then we came, and saw that it was there.

Unexpected till we came and saw it
Unbelievable as soon as seen
Hit the mark, despite not aiming for it:
Isn't that how things have always been?

PLEASURES

The first look out of the window in the morning
The old book found again
Enthusiastic faces
Snow, the change of the seasons
The newspaper
The dog
Dialectics
Taking showers, swimming
Old music
Comfortable shoes
Taking things in
New music
Writing, planting
Travelling
Singing
Being friendly.

TO EAT OF MEAT JOYOUSLY

To eat of meat joyously, a juicy loin cut
And with the fresh-baked, fragrant rye bread
Chunks from the whole cheese, and to swallow
Cold beer from the jug: such things are held in
Low esteem, but to my mind, to be put into the grave
Without ever enjoying a mouthful of good meat
Is inhuman, and I say that, I who
Am not good at eating.

THE ABANDONED GREENHOUSE

Exhausted from watering the fruit trees
I lately stepped through the open door into the small
    greenhouse

Where in the shadow of the tattered blind
Lie the remains of the rare flowers.

Still, made from wood, cloth and wire netting, stands
The installation, still the twine holds
The pale withered stems upright.
Bygone days' attention
Is still visible, many a subtle touch. Across the tented roof
Sways the shadow of the common evergreens
Which, living by rain, have no need of art.
As always the lovely and sensitive
Are no longer.

DIFFICULT TIMES

Standing at my desk
Through the window I see the elder tree in the garden
And recognise something red in it, something black
And all at once recall the elder
Of my childhood in Augsburg.
For several minutes I debate
Quite seriously whether to go to the table
And pick up my spectacles, in order to see
Those black berries again on their tiny red stalks.

THINGS CHANGE

I
And I was old, and I was young at moments
Was old at daybreak, young when darkness came
And was a child recalling disappointments
And an old man forgetting his own name.

II
Sad in my young days
Sad later on
When can I be happy?
Better be soon.

TO THE STUDENTS OF THE WORKERS' AND PEASANTS' FACULTY

1

So there you sit. And how much blood was shed
That you might sit there. Do such stories bore you?
Well, don't forget that others sat before you
Who later sat on people. Keep your head!

2

Your science will be valueless, you'll find
And learning will be sterile, if inviting
Unless you pledge your intellect to fighting
Against all enemies of all mankind.

3

Never forget that men like you got hurt
That you might sit here, not the other lot.
And now don't shut your eyes, and don't desert
But learn to learn, and try to learn for what.

COUNTER-SONG TO 'THE FRIENDLINESS OF THE WORLD'

So does that mean we've got to rest contented
And say 'That's how it is and always must be'
And spurn the brimming glass for what's been emptied
Because we've heard it's better to go thirsty?

So does that mean we've got to sit here shivering
Since uninvited guests are not admitted
And wait while those on top go on considering
What pains and joys we are to be permitted?

Better, we think, would be to rise in anger
And never go without the slightest pleasure
And, warding off those who bring pain and hunger
Fix up the world to live in at our leisure.

HA! HA! HA!, LAUGHED SOCRATES'S
CLIENTS

Ha! Ha! Ha!, laughed Socrates's clients
But one of the three Ha's
Made him think.

The Pyramid of Cheops has eleven errors
The Bible an infinite number
And Newton's Physics
Is full of superstition.

Couples on their way home from the cinema
Could teach
Romeo and Juliet a thing or two
While Azdak's father quite often
Took his son aback.

WHEN IN MY WHITE ROOM AT THE
CHARITÉ

When in my white room at the Charité
I woke towards morning
And heard the blackbird, I understood
Better. Already for some time

I had lost all fear of death. For nothing
Can be wrong with me if I myself
Am nothing. Now
I managed to enjoy
The song of every blackbird after me too.

AND I ALWAYS THOUGHT

And I always thought: the very simplest words
Must be enough. When I say what things are like
Everyone's heart must be torn to shreds.
That you'll go down if you don't stand up for yourself
Surely you see that.

Index of the titles in German

Chronological list of Poems

For 'Key to the Translators' see page 627.
Those translations which bear no translator's initials involve a degree of collaboration on the Editors' part which makes final responsibility difficult to establish.

* GW, Prosa I, *Me-ti*, p. 498

* See note on p. 586

KEY TO THE TRANSLATORS

EA	Edith Anderson	HAK	H. Arthur Klein
AB	Anya Bostock	LL	Lesley Lendrum
DB	Derek Bowman	PL	Peter Levi
EB	Eva Bornemann	CM	Christopher Middleton
LB	Lee Baxendall	HM	Humphrey Milnes
PB	Patrick Bridgwater	HBM	H. B. Mallalieu
SHB	Sidney H. Bremer	MM	Michael Morley
AC	Alasdair Clayre	RM	Ralph Manheim
JC	John Cullen	SMCL	Sammy McLean
RC	Robert Conard	KN	Karl Neumann
ME	Martin Esslin	ER	Edith Roseveare
AHM	Agnes Headlam-Morley	GR	Georg Rapp
HH	H. R. Hays	MR	Muriel Rukeyser
MH	Michael Hamburger	NR	Naomi Replansky
FJ	Frank Jellinek	SS	Stephen Spender
FJS	Frank Jones	JW	John Willett
NJ	Nicholas Jacobs	JFW	J. F. Williams